MW01534233

The Path Less Taken:
Immanent Critique in Curriculum and Pedagogy

Principal Author

James G. Henderson

Edited by

Jennifer L. Schneider

Felicia,
Brightest of
Blessings to you
always! :)
Jennifer
Schneider

Educator's International Press, Inc.
Troy, NY

James G. Henderson

The Path Less Taken: Immanent Critique in Curriculum and Pedagogy

Published by Educator's International Press, Inc.
18 Colleen Road
Troy, N.Y. 12180

Copyright © 2010 by Educator's International Press, Inc.

All rights reserved. No part of this publication may be produced or transmitted in any form or by any means, electronic or mechanical, including photocopying, or any information, storage and retrieval system, without permission from the publisher.

Library of Congress
Cataloging in Publication Division

Library of Congress
CIP 20540-4320

The Path Less Taken: Immanent Critique in Curriculum and Pedagogy / James G. Henderson

p. cm.

ISBN   1-891928-38-4

6   5   4   3   2   1
Manufactured in the United States of America

The Path Less Taken:

Immanent Critique in Curriculum and Pedagogy

Felicia,

Best wishes for you future,

creative C&P work.

Jim Henderson

Table of Contents

Epistemology and Curriculum Studies

PATRICK SLATTERY
Professor, Texas A&M University

MARK ORTWEIN
Doctoral Candidate, Texas A&M University

This collection of essays offers a fresh examination of the epistemological foundations of curriculum studies through the lens of the ten year history of the Curriculum and Pedagogy Conference and Publications. Curriculum and Pedagogy (C&P) was founded in 1999 by several professors and graduate students with the explicit intention of developing a scholarly community committed to investigating the connections between curriculum and pedagogy in the context of democratic spaces with transparent governance. The *Journal of Curriculum and Pedagogy (JCP)* — James Henderson and Patrick Slattery served as founding co-editors from 2004 through 2010 — was one of the major publications of C&P along with the Annual Conference Proceedings. Our Editors' Introductions to *JCP* over this six year period attempted to establish an epistemological framework for scholarship in the journal and in the curriculum field. We also intended to invite the entire curriculum field to reflect on the interrelationship of curriculum and pedagogy, as well as the ways that the mission of the organization informed democracy and transparency in *JCP*. Our Editors' Introductions are reprinted in this volume with the hope of providing a context to review and analyze our scholarly intent. We are pleased that many scholars from the C&P community have engaged our work in this collection and extend our concept of curriculum and pedagogy in their own unique and interesting ways.

The Curriculum and Pedagogy Group and the *JCP* were both outgrowths of and responses to other curriculum conferences of the 1980s and 1990s — particularly the Bergamo Conference on Curriculum Theory and Classroom Practice that had been an academic home for most of the professors who were involved in the founding of C&P. We were all indebted to the rich history of intellectual rigor at Bergamo, but we were also inspired to move beyond Bergamo and our perceived shortcomings of Bergamo. Many scholars and graduate students attend both C&P and Bergamo, and they published in both *JCP* and the *Journal of Curriculum Theorizing (JCT)*. It would be inaccurate to think of Bergamo and C&P as opposite or opposing organizations. It would also be incorrect to categorize scholars who publish in *JCP* or *JCT* as distinctly different. In fact, a quick review of program participants and journal publications will reveal more intersection than divergence. There remains a synergy in the curriculum field that traverses all conferences and journals including AERA Division B. However, with that said, it is accurate to reflect on the unique contributions of the mission and publications of C&P and *JCP* as we are doing in this collection of essays.

What is the nature of the epistemological assumptions of Curriculum and Pedagogy? The 1960s bore witness to dramatic and analogous cracks in the bed-rock assumptions of both educational theory and analytic epistemology. In the early 1960s, Edmond Gettier (1963), an American epistemologist, penned his landmark paper, *Is justified true belief knowledge?* Here he demonstrated that justified true belief—the definition of knowledge that had served philosophers for more than two millennia—could be undermined via cleverly constructed case studies. The initial response to these *Gettier Cases* in philosophy circles was disbelieving consternation. With time, however, it became increasingly clear that he had struck the discipline a severe blow. Philosophers responded with a flurry of counter-examples. "Epistemologists appeared to think that salvation from Gettier lay in fastidiousness and technical finery, so that epistemology became increasingly ingrown, epicyclical, and irrelevant to broader philosophical and human concerns" (Roberts & Wood, 2007, p. 5). Some critics even argued that traditional epistemology was gasping in final spasmodic breath (Williams, 1999).

Similarly, the 1960s and 70s were a tumultuous time in curriculum departments — a period that represents a radical shift away from the traditional understanding of the curriculum scholar's work and the foundation laid by Ralph Tyler (1949). Scientific management, behavioral objectives, and bureaucratic emphases seemed to have run its course (so we thought!), and the excitement of the Reconceptualization launched robust philosophical, theoretical, and literary analyses. In language echoing the "death of epistemology," Joseph Schwab (1969) declared the field "...moribund, unable to present methods and principles to continue its work and desperately in search of new and more effective principles and methods" (p. 1). William Pinar, among others, took this declaration seriously, and established the context for the robust changes of the 1970s and 80s. As we know, the Reconceptualization signaled the beginning of a new era of highly theoretical work in the curriculum field, drawing from a range of humanities based disciplines.

At least two analogies can be drawn. First, both the field of philosophy and the field of curriculum studies experienced foundational upheaval during roughly the same period of time—upheaval understood by their respective critics in the metaphorical language of death. A notable difference occurs in the initial responses of each field: where many curriculum theorists almost immediately embraced the intellectual liberty of the Reconceptualization, epistemologists were quite recalcitrant. By the 1980s, however, several respected epistemologists had broken ranks with the establishment. For generations, epistemology had limited its analysis to the *outward* properties of beliefs and had neglected the *inward* characteristics of the agents. The introduction of virtue epistemology in the 1980s marked a redirection of focus away from the sterile qualities and conditions for knowledge, and instead made the characteristics and dispositions of persons the subject of study (Battaly, 2010, p. 2). A similar and analogous shift occurred in curriculum theory. Maxine Greene's introduction of existential perspectives into the scholarly discourse, as well as the new emphasis on autobiographical research and psychoanalysis by Pinar, Janet Miller, and Madeleine Grumet, typifies the move from outward structural concerns associated with the Tylerian Rationale, to the inward-looking emphasis on subjective experience (Greene, 1974). It is in this space—some might call it a phenomenological epistemology—that C&P was birthed. With this collection, we now see the maturing of the Curriculum and Pedagogy movement and the establishment of the next phase of the curriculum field.

References

Battaly, H. (2010). Introduction: Virtue and vice. *Metaphilosophy, 41*(1-2), 1-21.

Gettier, E. L. (1963). Is justified true belief knowledge? *Analysis, 23*(6), 121-123.

Greene, M. (1974). *Teacher as stranger: Educational philosophy for the modern age.* Belmont, CA: Wadsworth Publishing Company.

Roberts, R. C., & Wood, W. J. (2007). *Intellectual virtues: An essay in regulative epistemology.* Oxford: Oxford University Press.

Schwab, J. J. (1969). The practical: A language for curriculum. *The School Review, 78*(1), 1-23.

Tyler, R. W. (1949). *Basic principles of curriculum and instruction.* Chicago: University of Chicago Press.

Williams, M. (1999). *Groundless belief: An essay on the possibility of epistemology.* Princeton: Princeton University Press.

The Path Less Taken: Immanent Critique in Curriculum and Pedagogy

JAMES G. HENDERSON
Kent State University

Is there any value in reprinting a set of essays I composed between May, 2004 and November, 2009 in the *Journal of Curriculum and Pedagogy (JCP)*? This was a question I had been pondering for several months before I finally decided to discuss this matter with Bill Clockel in June, 2010. Bill's company, Educator's International Press (EIP), had published the first twelve issues of *JCP*, from Volume 1, Number 1 in Summer 2004 through Volume 6, Number 2 in Winter 2009; and as co-editor of *JCP* during this time period, I had composed eleven essays addressing the interrelated mission statements that had been created by the Curriculum and Pedagogy (C&P) Group and by the initial *JCP* editorial staff. The website version of the C&P Group's mission statement is a short paragraph, while the *JCP* mission statement is an essay-length explication and exploration of this paragraph. The C&P Group's statement is reprinted here, and the longer *JCP* essay is attached as Appendix A at the end of this book:

> The Curriculum and Pedagogy group is a gathering of diverse individuals seeking academic enrichment, social action, and professional engagement. Our conference is an annual space where work can be shared, valued, and disseminated to a diverse audience committed to educational reform and social change. The conference creates democratic spaces to advance public moral leadership in education through dialogue and action. It is characterized by its commitment to classroom teachers, school administrators and curriculum workers and in providing a venue for under-represented groups. The conference organizers seek to bring together individuals from diverse settings, including school district curriculum leaders and K-12 teachers, non-governmental community groups and organizations, graduate students and scholars from public schools to universities who seek to integrate, interrogate, and develop curriculum and pedagogical theories into action for educational empowerment and social justice.

Understanding the C&P Mission

I began my phone meeting with Bill Clockel by sharing a personal story, which I repeat here. Back in 1999, I had conversation with Jim Sears, who is arguably the key founding figure of the C&P Group, about the importance of cultivating a deepening understanding of the C&P mission. My conversation with Jim revolved around an edited text that Kathleen Kesson and I had just completed on the topic of "understanding democratic curriculum leadership" (Henderson & Kesson, 1999). Gadamer's (1975) insights into practicing the "art" of interpretation informed this project. Though Gadamer's argument is subtle and complex, his main points are fairly commonsensical and can be briefly summarized. We human beings are naturally biased in our outlooks and do not automatically possess a deep understanding of any particular matter. Though we can never overcome our biases and claim 'objective' knowledge, we can broaden our individual "horizons" by engaging in an open-minded "play" of interpretations with diverse others. However, we can only do this if we are willing to examine our beliefs and challenge our ideological scripts. Seeking 'truth' requires a disciplined, open-minded, open-hearted dialogue and is quite different from following predetermined methods, procedures and/or rules. Seeking truth does not necessarily result in consensus; it may lead to disagreement. Such "egalitarian" dissensus (Rancière, 2010) is not necessarily a problem since the point of an open-ended, complicated conversation is to broaden personal horizons. If those engaged in the conversation are cultivating a deepening understanding of the topic under consideration, the dialogue is generative. If those enjoined in the dialogue are experiencing a sense of renewal, the dissensus is constructive and expansive, not delimiting and destructive. Rancière (2010) writes:

> It is possible to define a certain dissensual practice of philosophy as an activity of de-classification that undermines all policing of domains and formulas. It does so not for the sole pleasure of deconstructing the master's discourse, but in order to think the lines according to which boundaries and passages are constructed, according to which they are conceivable and modifiable. This critical practice of philosophy is an inseparable egalitarian, or anarchistic, practice since it considers arguments, narratives, testimonies, investigations and metaphors all as the equal inventions of a common capacity in a common language, Engaging in critique of the instituted divisions, then, paves the way for renewing our interrogations into what we are able to think and to do. (p. 218)

Jim Sears and I both felt that the C&P Group's sustainability—its vitality, strength, and durability—would, ultimately, depend on such a personal deepening of understanding of the C&P mission by all those involved in this somewhat fluid professional community. But would this rich and robust interpretive engagement take place? We pondered this question in 1999 and could only hope for the best positive outcome. Over the next few years, I continued to think about this personal and professional challenge; and as Patrick Slattery and I assumed the responsibilities of serving as the first co-editors of *JCP*, I told Patrick that I would like to incorporate my ongoing interpretations of the C&P/*JCP* mission statements into each issue's "Editors' Introduction." Patrick agreed that this would be a good idea, and we proceeded in a particular way.

Practicing Immanent Critique

I decided to create a clear and consistent focus for my interpretive essays, so I summarized the C&P/*JCP* mission statements as follows: *The C&P mission can be interpreted as advancing the synergistic relationship between disciplined curriculum studies, critical pedagogy and democratic educational leadership.* I composed each issue's interpretive essay with this focus in mind, sent the essay to Patrick for his feedback, and then incorporated the essay into the other sections of our Editors' Introduction. The only time I broke from this pattern was the Winter, 2007 issue of *JCP* (Volume 4, Number 2). I did not have time to compose a lengthy interpretive essay, so Patrick composed an opening two-paragraph statement on the continuing 'mission' discussion in our Editors' Introductions. The complete set of C&P/*JCP* mission interpretations, including Patrick's brief 4(2) statement, are reprinted as Part I of this book. This material has been slightly edited and rearranged from the original issues for purposes of continuity and coherence.

To return to the opening question in this introductory chapter, why bother with this reprinting effort? The interpretive perspectives have already been published, so is not this current textual project redundant? I will respond to these two questions by addressing a key assumption embedded in my Jim Sears story with an additional set of inquiries. Does the C&P Group's sustainability actually depend on cultivating a deepening personal understanding of its mission by all the community members? What if this interpretive, playful dialogue did not take place? Would it matter? What happens when members of any professional organization or, in a broader sense, citizens of any society do not cultivate a deepening personal understanding of the ideals they profess? Are they being morally and ethically lackadaisical? When humans do not continuously refine their individual moral compasses and when the cultivation of a sense of personal integrity is not a priority, what happens to their social relations? More specifically, with reference to the C&P Group, what ties the educational professionals who attend the annual meetings together? What drives C&P activities? Is it simply individual self-interest—what Dewey (1930/1999) characterizes as "old" individualism? Does the C&P Group exist mainly as a venue for conference presentations and peer-reviewed publications, particularly for newer members of the academy? Is "careerism" the tie that binds C&P? If so, how long will the C&P Group endure?

While working on my interpretations of the C&P mission and pondering such critical inquiries, I had a fortuitous conversation with Kent den Heyer at one of the annual C&P conferences in Marble Falls, Texas. He introduced me to Badiou's (2001) work on ethical fidelity. Badiou argues for a personal integrity that is grounded in "events" that inspire "for all" inclusiveness. Such an ethic is based on individual inspirations with universal implications. In effect, the personal is embedded in a "traversal of all differences" (Badiou, 2003, p. 110). Individual consciousness is stretched beyond tribal, ideological, national and other constraints. Badiou (2003) writes, "Thought is subjected to the ordeal of conformity, and only the universal, through an uninterrupted labor, an inventive traversal, relieves it" (p. 110). Badiou argues that we cannot reject our historical circumstances, but we can commit ourselves to a continuous, inclusive renewal. He writes, "It is always possible for a nonconformist thought to think in the century. This is what a subject is. It is he [or she] who maintains the universal, not conformity. Only what is in immanent exception is universal" (Badiou, 2003, pp. 110-111).

Badiou's ethical fidelity interjects an interesting and compelling possibility into the process of broadening horizons. When the play of individual understandings becomes inspired by universal "for all" thoughts and feelings, there is the potential for a qualitative shift in personal awareness. The meaning making can take on a deeper valence; a deepening mindfulness can enter the picture. A profound, powerful and "immanent" humanizing can pervade the process. Badiou describes how Saint Paul, the Jew, becomes inspired by Christ, the universal teacher. Paul does not reject his Jewishness, but he is no longer limited by that historical circumstance. Badiou (2003) writes, "The task Paul sets for himself is obviously not that of abolishing Jewish particularity, which he constantly acknowledges as the event's principle of historicity, but that of animating it internally by everything of which it is capable relative to the new discourse, and hence the new subject" (p. 103).

After reading a number of Badiou's philosophical essays, particularly his key text, *Being and Event*, I recognized that John Dewey's and Maxine Greene's personal yet interrelated journeys of understanding were, in effect, curriculum and teaching "events" that were inspiring my personal examinations of the C&P mission; and of course, I recognized that many other educators who were attending the C&P conferences were also personally inspired by Dewey and Greene. I was inspired by John Dewey in one way and by Maxine Greene in an overlapping but slightly different way, and I can best explain these interconnected dual inspirations in the context of discussing my position on "good" critical work. This is particularly relevant topic since the Editors' Introductions essays were written from a particular critical framework.

With reference to Fay's (1987) analysis of "fully developed" critical theory, I take the position that mature critique addresses two questions: *how do I establish critical distance from dehumanizing, debilitating personal and social phenomena in affirming ways; and how do I embody the changes that I seek?* Georg Wilhelm Friedrich (G. W. F.) Hegel's method of **"immanent critique"** informs these two questions. Good (2006) writes:

> Hegel intended the dialectic as a method of cultural criticism that identifies the standards of rationality within an existing culture or system of thought and then criticizes practices that do not accord with those standards of rationality. This method is immanent critique in the sense that it criticizes a culture on its own terms, on the basis of its highest ideals, rather than some apodictic first principle or transcendent, abstract moral standards." (p. 1)

Hegel's notion of **immanent critique** can be rephrased in more common, vernacular language as engaging in the challenge of 'walking one's talk,' 'speaking through one's deeds,' and 'practicing what one preaches.'

Applying Hegel's **immanent critique** to a "complicated conversation" (Pinar, 2004) about the C&P mission is quite challenging. What is the standard of rationality that underlies the C&P ideals? What is the most productive way to interpret C&P 'standards' and 'ideals?' Is this C&P soul-searching more about personal and professional dispositions and lifestyles? Can C&P standards and ideals be translated into objective criteria? What does it mean to actualize standards and embody ideals? What is the meaning of C&P integrity? How does the practice of **immanent critique** address internal psychological *and* external structural obstacles and constraints? How does one go about establishing critical distance from such barriers and blockages? These are very difficult, complex questions; and as I worked on the Editors' Introduction essays, I turned to Dewey and Greene for inspiration and guidance.

Good (2006) presents a vivid, thoughtful account of Dewey's personal journey to understand Hegel's **immanent critique** and to rethink Hegel's critical, dialectical approach in more pragmatic, accessible terminology. He concludes his narrative analysis with this comparative summary:

> Like, Hegel, Dewey always eschewed reductive and dualistic explanations in favor of a holistic approach in which the parts are seen as functions within a dynamic whole. He called for continual human growth through self-development, and employed a Hegelian method of immanent cultural criticism. Like Hegel..., Dewey continued to reject the Enlightenment tendency to reduce experience to cognition, and in fact he developed that theme most fully in *Experience and Nature* and *Art as Experience*, by arguing for the aesthetic nature of experience. He continued to examine experience in its organic wholeness, rather than as raw material in need of intellectual synthesis. Experience, for Dewey, does not need to be constructed out of a mass of disconnected sense data; rather, it needs to be analyzed, reconstructed and thus directed, when possible, toward desirable ends. ...Dewey continued to understand logic as a theory of learning rather than proof, and thus as a critical tool of human growth or self-development. Self development for both [Hegel and Dewey]...is a striving toward one's potential, but it also includes positive freedom, understood as liberation through commitment to one's social responsibilities, and recognition of our worth by our peers. (Good, 2006, p. 246)

Good's main point is that Hegel's notion of **immanent critique** was reframed by Dewey as holistic, "educative" experience (Dewey, 1938/1998).

Establishing a Critical Referent

As I worked on the Editors' Introduction essays, I decided that my 'standard of rationality' would be Dewey's conception of experience, particularly as interpreted in two books that I had co-authored: *Curriculum Wisdom* (Henderson & Kesson, 2004) and *Transformative Curriculum Leadership* (Henderson & Gornik, 2007). The centrality of these two co-authored texts will be quite apparent in the Part I material. Both books carefully establish critical distance from "reductive and dualistic explanations" in education. *Curriculum Wisdom* invites the cultivation of a love of democratic wisdom through the practice of "arts of inquiry," while *Transformative Curriculum Leadership* invites critically-informed educators to initiate and sustain four interrelated transactions: rethink educational standards in holistic terms, inquire into the experiential learning implications, engage in the necessary deliberative artistry, undertake the required personal journeys of understanding as "lead learners" (Barth, 2008) who initiate and facilitate supportive learning communities and public intellectual projects.

Through his highly productive academic and public intellectual career, Dewey consistently declared his faith that, with the proper educational support, *all* humans can refine and realize their 'democratic' identity and that through this actualization, "deep democracy" (Green, 1999) gradually emerges. It is worth quoting Dewey at some length on his faith in this personal development since it goes to the heart of his approach to **immanent critique**. Dewey (1888/1997) writes:

> Aristocracy and democracy both imply that the actual state of society exists for the sake of realizing an end which is ethical, but aristocracy implies that this is to be done primarily by means of special institutions or organizations within society, while democracy holds that the ideal is already at work in every personality, and must be trusted to care for itself. There is an individualism in democracy which there is not in aristocracy; but it is an ethical, not numerical individualism; it is an individualism of freedom, of responsibility, of initiative to and for the ethical ideal, not an individualism of lawlessness. In one word, democracy means that *personality* is the first and final reality. ...The spirit of personality indwells in every individual and that the choice to develop it must proceed from that individual. From this central position of personality result the other notes of democracy, liberty, equality, fraternity—words which are not mere words to catch the mob, but symbols of the highest ethical idea which humanity has yet reached—the idea that personality is the one thing of permanent and abiding worth and that in every human individual there lies personality. ...The best test of any form of society is the ideal with it proposes for the forms of its life, and the degree in which it realize this ideal. (pp. 199, 204)

My Editors' Introduction essays resonate with Dewey's faith in the possibilities for this personal growth—this holistic development-from-within. In effect, I take the position that the practice of a particular art of understanding will, over-time, result in the emergence of more democratic structures. The personal does not cause the social—they are inextricably interrelated; but holistically maturing personalities lead the way. Such individuals are the lead learners for a democratic way of life. Their emerging consciousness is a key catalyst for democratically progressive ends-in-view. Dewey (1888/1997) declares:

> The true meaning of equality is synonymous with the definition of democracy.... It is the form of society in which every man [and woman] has a chance and knows that he [or she] has it—and we may add, a chance to which no possible limits can be put, a chance which is truly in-

finite, the chance to become a person. Equality, in short, is the ideal of humanity; an ideal in the consciousness of which democracy lives and moves. (p. 201)

I place my trust in holistic, lead-learner initiatives for transformative curriculum and teaching practices, and I find that Maxine Greene embodies this critical orientation (Henderson, 2010). In fact, Greene's work was a continuous source of stimulation, provocation and awakening as I composed my Editors' Introduction essays. In a concluding statement in an edited book celebrating her career, she writes that, "I am not yet;" and adds:

> Inspiration…is not the exclusive privilege of poets and artists. …Teaching, writing, speaking, looking at paintings, watching plays and dance performances, listening to music, reading (always reading), I know the challenges are always new. The questions still gather, and I relish my sense of incompleteness. I can only live it seems to me, with a consciousness of possibility, of what might be, of what *ought* to be. Looking back, I attribute my choosing of questions to my being a woman (and a wife and mother), to my involvement with literature and the other arts, to the persisting conversations with students, to my friendships, and to my awareness of the darkness, of the silence that greets or longing for some cosmic meaning, for a 'truth'. (Greene, 1998, p. 256)

Greene (1988) notes that conversations about democracy and education can never, "be finished or complete. There is always more. There is always possibility. And this is where the space opens for the pursuit of freedom" (p. 128). She presents a complex, layered understanding of human liberation: "Freedom cannot be conceived apart from a matrix of social, economic, cultural, and psychological conditions" (Greene, 1988, p. 80). She further understands that this understanding of human freedom demands a sophisticated practical wisdom—a flexible, reflective practice informed by a balanced critical awareness. She argues that the "consequences of free action…are to a large degree unpredictable" (p. 46). Engaging in our best practical intelligence is "the price we must pay" for democratic pluralism (p. 46). Affirming Dewey's pragmatic interpretation of Hegel's **immanent critique**, Greene (1988) writes:

> Dewey…grew up in the Hegelian stream; and the Hegelian view of dialectical change and development remained alive in his thinking. What he rejected in time, however, was the idea of the World Spirit, the Absolute, the cosmic order. …The Hegelian view that autonomy and freedom are attained when human beings grasp, through the exercise of reason, the overarching order of things was revised. For Dewey, there was no cosmic purpose fulfilling itself in history. Nonetheless, there was a clear

connection between identity and what he called the "freed intelligence" necessary for direction of freedom of action. (pp. 42-43)

Based on Dewey's rethinking of the Hegelian heritage, Greene advances a subtle "dialectical" understanding of human freedom through a careful balancing of structural critique and existential affirmation. Her critique focuses on "oppression or exploitation or segregation or neglect" (Greene, 1988, p. 9). Through disciplined critical work, people can establish distance from their psychological and/or social shackles; they can responsibly express "the right not to be interfered with or coerced or compelled to do what [one] did not choose to do" (Greene, 1988, p. 16). This is the *freedom from* side of the dialectic. Greene then celebrates authentic self-direction. This is the *freedom to* side of her dialectic, and it refers to the ultimate fruition of democratic emancipation: "freedom shows itself or comes into being when individuals come together in a particular way, when they are authentically present to one another (without masks, pretenses, badges of office), when they have a project they can mutually pursue" (Greene, 1988, p. 16). Authentic, responsible self-direction is directed toward a "carnival" of creative human expressions (Sidorkin, 1999), which culminates in a robust cultural renaissance that replaces unimaginative standardization and political correctness.

Greene (1988) describes a variety of forms of oppression, exploitation, segregation, and neglect in American society. Not only those associated with our dehumanizing racist, sexist, classist, and homophobic heritage but with more subtle forms such as "constraining family rituals," "bureaucratic supervisory systems," and, ironically, static images of "freedom" that serve the interests of the wealthy, the powerful and the ideologically rigid (Greene, 1988, p. 17). She recognizes that struggles against freedom's constraints must be broad-based and multi-leveled. She summarizes her understanding of human freedom by acknowledging the intimate relationship between personal and social emancipation:

> On the one hand, [my] quest has been deeply personal: that of a woman striving to affirm the feminine as wife, mother, and friend, while reaching, always reaching, beyond the limits imposed by the obligations of a woman's life. On the other hand, it has been in some sense deeply public as well: that of a person struggling to connect the undertaking of education, with which she has been so long involved, to the making and remaking of a public space, a space of dialogue and possibility. (Greene, 1988, p.xi)

I view Dewey's and Greene's philosophical projects as vivid illustrations of Fay's (1987) "fully developed" critical theorizing. Both educational philosophers establish critical distance from dehumanizing, debilitating personal and/or social phenomena in affirming ways and embody the changes that they seek. I view their similarly balanced but personally distinctive approaches as exemplifying the 'path less taken' in critical work. Too many humans do not engage in self-examination, nor do they practice constructive criticism. They readily, and perhaps justifiably, find fault with other individuals, with other ideological camps, and/or with deeply embedded social structures in their society or other societies. However, they too quickly send the message: 'the trouble with you is…' or 'the trouble with society is…' without considering how they might be part of the problem. They criticize without personal introspection, self-examination, soul-searching. And they criticize without offering hopeful solutions. They are clear about what they are against but not about what they stand for, particularly for all of humanity. What is their sense of positive freedom for all? What are the universal values that they affirm, and how will others learn to embody these values? Finally, how will these critics work as 'lead learners' who embody the changes that they seek?

Introducing the Book's Title

The book's title, *The Path Less Taken*, refers to limited practice of immanent critique in our current historical moment. The title also highlights the curricular nature of immanent critique since the Latin term, "curriculum," etymologically denotes educational courses of action. Less taken "paths" are not well-marked, well-established, linear phenomena. Engaging in such educational journeying is an exploratory, meandering, and creative undertaking. The book's subtitle, *Immanent Critique in Curriculum and Pedagogy*, communicates the critical and substantive focus of this text. John Dewey's and Maxine Greene's philosophical projects served as inspirations for this focus; and though I am equally inspired by both educational philosophers, I do think Greene's existential approach balances Dewey's more communitarian emphasis. As I have noted, the starting point for my Editors' Introduction essays was Gadamer's philosophical hermeneutics with his focus on the personal broadening of horizons through 'playful' dialogue. I think Gadamer maintains a good balance between the personal and the social in his way, as does Greene in her way. I worry that Dewey's work might be used to stress the social over the personal, the cultural over the individual; and when this occurs, the notion of immanent critique can recede from view.

I am concerned about this question of balance as I ponder the future of the C&P Group. I worry that too much emphasis on establishing a collective C&P identity might work against practicing the art of personal understanding, particularly with reference to undertaking creative initiatives.

Group understanding—the wisdom of the crowd—can be as narrow and oppressive as any unexamined personal interpretation. The 'horizons' of a group are only as good as the individual understandings of the members of that group. Peer review is not automatically 'democratic.' In fact, such terms as "democracy," "curriculum," "criticism," "pedagogy," and "leadership" have no essential meaning. There is no easy way to understand the *synergistic relationship between disciplined curriculum studies, critical pedagogy and democratic educational leadership*. The art of interpretation must be practiced, and the practice of this art has personal and social dimensions.

This book project has been conceived in the spirit of Maxine Greene's "positive" freedom. It is based on my personal initiative as an exercise in authentic engagement between voluntary adults. A prospectus of the text was not submitted for an "official" C&P Group peer review, and this generated some concerns in that professional community that were shared through a set of emails. There was not a final resolution on this matter; no consensus was achieved. Hopefully, however, all involved in this communication experienced a broadening of their personal horizons on what it means to be a 'member' of the C&P Group. If the email communications resulted in feelings of disconnection and alienation, that outcome would be contrary to the purpose of this book. This text has been designed to facilitate immanent critique in curriculum and pedagogy work. This is a very challenging undertaking for the C&P Group, for any educational organization or, in broadest possible terms, for the planet as a whole.

Providing an Overview of the Text

The Part II perspectives in this book extend the Part I Editors' Introduction essays in a very important way. While writing the essays that appear in Part I, I wondered what I would learn if I engaged in real-time, face-to-face interactions over what I was composing. Would my 'horizons' be broadened? If so, how? I was writing to invite conversation; but beyond Patrick's input, I was not engaged in any specific dialogue on the C&P/JCP mission statements. This is, of course, one of the downsides to academic writing. It is often the case that we academics publish material for which we do not get immediate feedback. We often wonder, "Is anybody reading the stuff that I am writing?" This book is designed, in part, to address this limitation. Since I was familiar with the "Perspectives" section in *JCP* and since Patrick and I received consistently good feedback on the addition of that section in each journal issue, I wanted to apply that successful format to this book's topic. Patrick and I created *JCP*'s "Perspectives" section for two reasons. We wanted to highlight the multitextual nature of curriculum and pedagogy topics (Pinar, Reynolds, Slattery, & Taubman, 1995), and we wanted to incorporate a textual application of town meeting dialogue. We designed the Perspectives section to function as a kind of simulated conversation on a particular question.

The Part II perspectives are written by a group of past and present leaders of the C&P organization. They present their interpretations of the C&P/*JCP* mission statements as part of a text-based, simulated town hall meeting on the topic of fidelity to the C&P mission. Due to the way I envisioned Part II, I asked Louise Allen if she would be willing to contribute a piece on the history of C&P town meetings. She agreed, and I think her essay provides an important historical context for the Part II perspectives. All of the contributors to this section of the book were asked to respond to a specific writing prompt; and they were told that their response could be an essay, a personal letter, a poem, or any other format that they found to be relevant and compelling. Here is their writing prompt:

> The C&P mission can be succinctly interpreted as advancing the synergistic relationship between disciplined curriculum studies, critical pedagogy and democratic educational leadership. This requires critically-informed educators to cross curriculum, teaching and leadership boundaries in bureaucratically compartmentalized P-12 settings and academically balkanized higher education settings. How do you understand the challenges of enacting this professional vision with ethical fidelity? Stated in a more vernacular way, how can critically-informed educators 'walk' this synergistic mission talk? How can they embody the holistic, integrated change that they seek?

The Part II perspectives will be followed by a concluding chapter; and like this introductory chapter, it has been composed as a personal essay. I will discuss the value of 'immanent' critical work for self-defined "Curriculum & Instruction" (C&I), Curriculum & Teaching (C&T), Curriculum & Pedagogy (C&P), Curriculum & Leadership (C&L) and Teaching, Curriculum, and Leadership Studies (TCLS) higher education units in the United States and around the world. Do these couplings exist for administrative convenience only, or are these terms linked though a commitment to an underlying professional mission? If it is the former situation, why is there not a mission statement; and what are the consequences of this lack of professional vision? If it is the latter circumstance, is the mission statement simply gathering dust in some file; and if so, what are the consequences of this lack of visionary attention?

I will discuss these questions in the context of two narratives. During the 2007-2009 academic years, the Teaching, Leadership and Curriculum Studies (TLCS) departmental faculty who taught courses in Kent State

University's C&I Master's Degree Program created a professional standard linking curriculum, teaching and democratic educational leadership. I will tell the story of how this work was accomplished in the context of the continuous, state-mandated North Central Association for Teacher Education (NCATE) evaluation of teacher education at Kent State. During the 2009-2010 academic year, Kent State's TCLS department received a $100,000 grant from the Ohio Department of Education to design and implement a pilot Teacher Leader Endorsement Program (TLEP). This is potentially significant ground-breaking work since Ohio is the first state in the United States to provide formal policy support for teacher leadership. I will tell the story of this pilot program, which involves eighteen experienced teachers in the suburban Cuyahoga Falls City School District.[1] This group of state-designated "teacher leaders" undertook a particular immanent critique of their school district's mission statement and then created collaborative leadership plans based on this critical work.

I will conclude this book by challenging higher education professors and P-12 teachers and their administrators to consider the vital importance of incorporating immanent critiques of their organizational mission statements into their work. If educators are not concerned about the ethical integrity of their work, what are the implications for their profession? If Hegel's idealizing, Dewey's experiencing and Greene's "I am not yet" are not part of educators' personal horizons, how can they argue that their profession is a vocational calling and not a job requiring strict management accountability? How can educators realize Dewey's vision for progressive education, "The art of thus giving shape to human powers and adapting them to social service is the supreme art; one calling into its service the best of artists; that no insight, sympathy, tact, executive power, is too great for such service" (Dewey 1897/2009, p. 40)?

References

Badiou, A. (2001). *Ethics: An essay on the understanding of evil* (P. Hallward, Trans.). London: Verso.

Badiou, A. (2003). *Saint Paul: The foundation of universalism* (R. Brassier, Trans.). Stanford, CA: Stanford University Press.

Badiou, A. (2005). *Being and event* (O. Feltham, Trans.). New York: Continuum.

Barth, R. S. (2008). Foreword. In G. A. Donaldson, *How leaders learn: Cultivating capacities for school improvement* (pp. ix-xi). New York: Teachers College Press.

---

[1] Cuyahoga Falls is a suburb of Akron, Ohio.

Dewey, J. (1997). The ethics of democracy. In L. Menand (Ed.), *Pragmatism: A reader* (pp. 182-204). New York: Vintage Books. (Original work published 1888)

Dewey, J. (1998). *Experience and education*. West Lafayette, IN: Kappa Delta Pi. (Original work published 1938)

Dewey, J. (1999). *Individualism old and new*. Amherst, NY: Prometheus Books. (Original work published 1929)

Dewey, J. (2009). My pedagogic creed. In D. J. Flinders & S. J. Thornton (Eds.), *The curriculum studies reader* (3rd ed., pp. 34-41). New York: Routledge. (Original work published 1897)

Fay, B. (1987). *Critical social science: Liberation and its limits*. Ithaca, NY: Cornell University Press.

Gadamer, H. G. (1975). *Truth and method* (G. Barden & J. Cumming, Eds. & Trans.). New York: Seabury.

Good, J. A. (2006). *A search for unity in diversity: The "permanent Hegelian deposit" in the philosophy of John Dewey*. Lanham, MD: Lexington Books.

Green, J. M. (1999). *Deep democracy: Community, diversity, and transformation*. Lanham, MD: Rowman & Littlefield.

Greene, M. (1988). *The dialectic of freedom*. New York: Teachers College Press.

Greene, M. (1998). Toward beginnings. In W. F. Pinar (Ed.), *The passionate mind of Maxine Greene: 'I am…not yet.'* (pp. 256-257). London: Falmer Press.

Henderson, J. G. (2010). Thanks, Maxine: From critical awareness to wide-awakeness. In R. Lake (Ed.), *Dear Maxine: Letters from the unfinished conversation* (pp.132-134). New York: Teacher College Press.

Henderson, J. G., & Gornik, R. (2007). *Transformative curriculum leadership* (3rd ed.). Upper Saddle River, NJ: Merrill/Prentice Hall.

Henderson, J. G., & Kesson, K. R. (Eds.). (1999). *Understanding democratic curriculum leadership*. New York: Teachers College Press.

Henderson, J. G., & Kesson, K. R. (2004). *Curriculum wisdom: Educational decisions in democratic societies*. Upper Saddle River, NJ: Merrill/Prentice Hall.

Pinar, W. F. (2004). *What is curriculum theory?* Mahwah, New Jersey: Erlbaum Associates.

Pinar, W. F., Reynolds, W. M., Slattery, P., & Taubman, P. M. (1995). *Understanding curriculum: An introduction to the study of historical and contemporary curriculum discourses*. New York: Peter Lang.

Rancière, J. (2010). *Dissensus: On politics and aesthetics* (S. Corcoran, Ed. & Trans.). London: Continuum.

Sidorkin, A. M. (1999). *Beyond discourse: Education, the self, and dialogue*. Albany, NY: State University of New York Press.

Part One

Situating the Editors' Introductions

JENNIFER L. SCHNEIDER
Kent State University

As the Spring 2010 semester at Kent State University was coming to a close, I received an invitation to participate in what for me would become my first steps on a new journey. The invitation was extended to me during a weekly meeting with Jim Henderson to discuss matters related to my graduate assistantship. After sharing his initial ponderings around creating a book to celebrate the 10th anniversary of the Curriculum & Pedagogy Group, which had been marked by a special event at the 2009 Conference in Atlanta, he asked if I would be interested in participating in this project as an editor. As a doctoral student eager to develop her scholarly-self, I graciously accepted the learning opportunity. Since the book would be designed to invite conversations about immanent critique in curriculum and pedagogy and to encourage educators to engage such critiques, we decided not to simply reprint the Editors' Introductions from the *Journal of Curriculum and Pedagogy (JCP)* verbatim. Consequently, over the course of this past summer, I reworked the first six years of *JCP* Editors' Introductions, form Volume 1, Number 1 to Volume 6, Number 2, with an eye toward supporting the book's two goals.

The best way to describe my process of editing the introductions would be that it was recursive in nature. I began with an initial read through of all of the Editors' Introduction essays noting key points, questions, and reactions to their content. Early on I noticed that the essays had a particular aesthetic flow, a certain ethical sensibility. During subsequent readings, I experienced an organic evolution in my thinking. I allowed space for my understanding of the essays to develop overtime and became aware that the *JCP* was an embodied of, and exploration into, issues surrounding democratic integrity.

Certain themes began to emerge during my growth of understanding, so I decided to organize the content from each Editors' Introduction around these thematic motifs. For the most part, I removed much of the written content summarizing the authors' articles; however, when it seemed pertinent and helped illumined the themes, I chose to leave in some content about contributors' manuscripts. I later translated these themes into the subtitles for this section of the book. In the spirit of Pinar's (2004) curriculum as *currere*, Jim and I decided to begin each subtitle with an infinitive form of a verb as a way of inviting new interpretations and personalized meanings by those who read the essays. The subtitles found on the pages to come include: *Celebrating Artistry in Curriculum and Pedagogy* (Volume 1, Number 1); *Studying Curriculum and Pedagogy Historically* (Volume 1, Number 2); *Pushing Beyond Social Engineering* (Volume 2, Number 1); *Examining Democracy, Spirituality, and Ethics in C&P* (Volume 2, Number 2); *Committing to Democratic Spaces in C&P* (Volume 3, Number 1); *Supporting the Process of Becoming/Knowing/Doing* (Volume 3, Number 2); *Discussing Ethical Challenges in Curriculum and Pedagogy* (Volume 4, Number 1); *Understanding Curriculum Leadership* (Volume 4, Number 2); *Advancing Three Disciplinary Dimensions of Curriculum-Based Pedagogy* (Volume 5, Number 1); *Evaluating a Pragmatic Understanding of Artistry, Development, and Leadership* (Volume 5, Number 2); *Exploring an Evolving Field* (Volume 6, Number 1); and *Concluding Thoughts and Reflections* (Volume 6, Number 2). Whether viewed collectively or individually, I see the essays in Part I of this book to be a living example of immanent critique applied to the work of curriculum and pedagogy.

How does one enter into a 'conversation' that went on for six years without having been part of that dialogue? I have continuously grappled with this question while working with these introductions because prior to starting this book project I had very little knowledge about the *JCP* and C&P Group. Even though I oversaw the majority of editorial matters like organizing the book, proofreading and copyediting manuscripts, and communicating with the contributors and publisher, working on this book has engaged me in a process of learning through inquiry. I have been introduced to the "complicated conversation" (Pinar, Reynolds, Slattery, & Taubman, 1995) that surrounds curriculum studies and begun to conceive of the curriculum studies through Pinar's (2007) disciplinarities of verticality and horizontality. I am not only beginning to make sense of the curriculum studies' "intellectual history" (p. xiii) and the foundational scholars in Jim's argument for immanent critique, but I am simultaneously gaining exposure to the field's "present intellectual circumstance" (p. xiv). To conclude, working on the creation of Part I in this book has invited me to converse with other educators who, like me, choose to walk along the path less taken as presented in this book.

References

Pinar, W. F. (2007). *Intellectual advancement through disciplinarity: Verticality and horizontality in curriculum studies.* Rotterdam: Sense Publishers.

Pinar, W. F., Reynolds, W. M., Slattery, P., & Taubman, P. M. (1995). *Understanding curriculum: An introduction to the study of historical and contemporary curriculum discourses.* New York: Peter Lang.

Pinar, W. F. (2004). *What is curriculum theory?* Mahwah, NJ: Lawrence Erlbaum Associates.

Celebrating Artistry in Curriculum and Pedagogy

Having served as the first co-editors of the *Journal of Curriculum and Pedagogy (JCP)*, we, James G. Henderson and Patrick Slattery, felt a great deal of satisfaction and joy in our role. The first issue was the culmination of years of determined work by a core of dedicated curriculum and teaching colleagues, and we feel honored and fortunate to have worked with them. What brought all of us together was the recognition that education is a form of human artistry that is, at its core, a curriculum-based pedagogy. This recognition requires educators to not only think deeply about what they teach but about how they go about their teaching and why they teach in the ways that they do. We agree with John Dewey (1887/1987) that when educators approach their work in this deeply thoughtful way, they are practicing the 'supreme' human art:

> The community's duty to education is its paramount moral duty... Through education, society can formulate its own purposes, can organize its own means and resources, and thus shape itself with definiteness and economy in the direction it wishes to move... Education thus conceived marks the most perfect and intimate union of science and art conceivable in human experience. The art of thus giving shape to human powers and adapting them to social service is the supreme art, one calling into its service the best of artists; that no insight, sympathy, tact, executive power, is too great for such a service. The teacher is engaged, not simply is the training of individuals, but in the formation of the proper social life. Every teacher should realize the dignity of his [or her] calling; that he [or she] is a social servant set apart for the maintenance of proper social order and the securing of the right social growth. (Dewey, 1897/1997, p. 23)

Though John Dewey wrote these words more than one hundred years ago, the education profession is, in general, not living up to this professional standard and calling; and this is, we believe, where the *JCP* enters the picture.

Each issue of the journal was an attempt to advance and celebrate the art of education through the recognition that this professional artistry is positioned at the intersection of the study and practice of curriculum and teaching. It is deeply unfortunate that current educational policies and structures generally separate curriculum and teaching inquiries, decisions, and actions. This results in an education profession (or should we say semi-profession?) that is overly managed and narrowly technical. Hence, the purpose of the journal was to critique this current historical situation and to offer creative solutions. To use a medical metaphor to help illustrate this point, the educational patient is sick due to an unhealthy lifestyle, and the patient will only recover when that way of living is altered. To attempt to solve the problem through the use of one quick-fix 'pill' (should we say fad?) after another is not to understand the problem. How much money must be spent on these pills before this is recognized?

Fortunately, there are many critically insightful educators in the United States, Canada, Mexico, Australia, and other countries who do recognize the vital necessity of practicing a curriculum and pedagogy lifestyle. They work in all kinds of settings, including public and private schools, small colleges and large universities, museums, urban centers, rural co-ops, and diverse service organizations. There are many educators who manage to work in imaginative and thoughtful ways despite our current historical conditions and that was clearly exemplified in the very first Summer 2004 issue with Dana Keller and Kathleen Kesson's exchange, Sheri Leafgren and Debra DeBenedictus' insights, Linda Wolf and Diane Craig's personal reflections, Stephanie Springgay's arts-based educational research (ABER), Nancy J. Brooks and Thomas S. Poetter's discussion of moral direction for the field of curriculum studies, and the eclectic array of sixteen curriculum scholars and leaders from various institutional and international settings providing glimpses into the current state of curriculum studies and teaching environments. Wherever education is practiced, there are passionate, deeply caring educational artists; and the *JCP* is, ultimately, dedicated to all of them. It is a space committed to describing, advancing, and celebrating these professionals and their scholarship.

In order to facilitate a space for rich and complex investigations of curriculum and pedagogy in our contemporary schools and society, the design of the *JCP* was intended to simulated dialogue and to show the multitextual nature of curriculum and pedagogy. The Editors' Introductions not only sought to introduce each issue's contributors but were also written with the continuous grounding focus being the C&P and *JCP* mission statements. Since art can be provocative, inspire, lift the soul, and challenge the intellect, every issue of *JCP* featured arts-based educational research and challenging images related to curriculum and pedagogy. Examples of these included, but were not limited to, Volume 1, Number 2 where the creative, brilliant art education scholar and artist B. Stephen Carpenter, II explored the integral connection between the arts and curriculum and pedagogy, and Volume 2, Number 1 where Johnny Saldaña shared his ethnodramatic piece entitled *Street rat: An ethnodrama*, which focused on homeless youth in New Orleans.

The second portion of every issue of the *JCP* was dedicated to various perspectives from those within the curriculum studies community. Each issue a question related to curriculum and pedagogy was posed to a broad range of scholars, practitioners, teachers, and graduate students. Some of the questions posed over the past six years included: How can the arts inspire curriculum and pedagogy synergy? (Volume 1, Number 1); What recent developments have you experienced in Gay, Lesbian, Bisexual, Transgender, Intersex, and Queer (GLBTIQ) Studies, Queer Theory Courses, and Gay-Straight Alliances in Schools and Universities? (Volume 4, Number 2); What is Curriculum Studies? (Volume, 5, Number 2); and What are the resulting implications if we continue to treat curriculum/teaching theory and practice as separate domains of academic research? (Volume 4, Number 1). The purpose of the Perspectives essays as well as the articles in the journal was to represent diverse voices and profound insights into the artistry in education.

Reference

Dewey, J. (1997). My pedagogic creed. In D. J. Flinders & S. J. Thornton (Eds.), *The curriculum studies reader* (pp. 17-23). New York: Routledge. (Original work published 1897)

Studying Curriculum and Pedagogy Historically

This is an exciting time to be a student of curriculum and pedagogy. Over the past thirty-five years, the curriculum field has advanced in several significant ways, and this journal is an important part of this story. We live in a historical period where those who are disciplined about curriculum work must be critically alert, but with a sense of pride. Curriculum workers today can walk with their heads high. There is much to feel good about, and we wish to present a brief narrative that provides a historical context for understanding this journal's significance and the relevance of this issue's Perspectives section on the arts.

Our story begins in 1969 with the publication of Joseph Schwab's first "practical" essay, which is entitled, *The Practical: A Language for Curriculum* (Schwab, 1969). The text Understanding Curriculum notes this date in a dramatic way:

> The main [curriculum] concepts today are quite different from those which grew out of an era in which school buildings and populations were growing exponentially, and when keeping the curriculum ordered and organized were the main motives of professional activity. That was a time of curriculum development. Curriculum development: Born: 1918. Died: 1969. (Pinar, Reynolds, Slattery, & Taubman, 1995, p. 6)

The 1918 date refers to the publication of Franklin Bobbitt's The Curriculum. Bobbitt was a Professor of Educational Administration at the University of Chicago, and his book is the first publication of a "synoptic" curriculum text in American education. As Pinar (2004) notes, this type of text is designed to "summarize curriculum scholarship and suggest its significance" (p. 7). Bobbitt (1918) organized this synoptic task around the advocacy of a particular protocol for curriculum development. Many other educators followed in Bobbitt's footsteps by advancing their own protocols. The most visible of these procedural texts was Ralph Tyler's Basic Principles of Curriculum and Instruction (1949). Tyler's curriculum development "rationale" can be read as a refinement of Bobbitt's protocol (Kliebard, 1975/1997).

There were, certainly, educational scholars who challenged this administrative, procedural approach to the study of curriculum, including Harold Rugg, George Counts, and Theodore Brameld (Stanley, 1992). These educators approached their work from a particular critical perspective; in effect, they worked within the confines of a specific theoretical orientation. Joseph Schwab, who was a colleague of Ralph Tyler's at the University of Chicago, was disturbed by the narrowness of the theoretical and the procedural approaches. He felt that both strategies missed the mark. Neither the critical theorists nor the proceduralists were working the way curriculum scholars should work. Neither properly understood the discipline of curriculum studies, so Schwab composed an essay which he first presented at an annual meeting of the American Educational Research Association (AERA) and for which he received an unusual standing ovation. In this essay, he makes two basic points. The phenomena of "curriculum," referring to educational courses of action that facilitate human "growth," is so complex that it cannot be studied through any particular theoretical perspective — no matter how critically insightful. Curriculum scholars must be theoretically sophisticated; they must approach their discipline eclectically. Schwab (1969/2000) writes:

> All the social and behavioral sciences are marked by "schools" each distinguished by a different choice of principle of enquiry, each of which selects from the intimidating complexities of the subject matter the small fraction of the whole with which it can deal. The theories which arise from enquiries so directed are, then, radically incomplete... It follows, then, that such theories are not, and will not be, adequate by themselves to tell us what to do with human beings or how to do it. What they variously suggest and the contrary guidance they afford to choice and action must be mediated and combined by eclectic arts... (p. 98)

His advocacy for the "arts of the eclectic" in curriculum work leads directly to his second point. He argues that this eclectic approach culminates in "arts of the practical," which are deliberative in nature and cannot be reduced to precise protocols. In effect, Schwab argued that the field of curriculum is disciplined in two specific ways, and his organizing terms for these two key disciplinary characteristics of the field were: arts of the eclectic and arts of the practical. The curriculum field is neither theoretical nor practical. It is both.

Though Schwab extends his 1969 argument into three additional essays that are published between 1971 and 1983 (Schwab, 1971, 1973, & 1983), his first essay is the ground breaking one. We celebrate its publication, and we wish we were in attendance at the annual AERA meeting when he presented his argument so that we could join in the standing ovation. We feel that his essay is, perhaps, the key moment in the disciplinary "birthing" of the curriculum field; and in fact, we would argue that until 1969, educators who were studying curriculum matters were not yet functioning as disciplined curriculum scholars simply because they did not, as yet, understand the disciplinary nature of their chosen field.

We now move to 1979, which is the publication of Elliot Eisner's *The educational imagination*. Eisner received his Ph.D. from the University of Chicago, and Joseph Schwab was one of his doctoral advisors. Working from Schwab's arts of the eclectic perspective, Eisner explores the arts of the practical in curriculum work through his organizing term of educational imagination. He writes:

> Teaching can be done as badly as anything else. It can be wooden, mechanical, mindless, and wholly unimaginative. But when it is sensitive, intelligent, and creative — those qualities that confer upon it the status of an art — it should, in my view, not be regarded as it so often is by some, as an

expression of unfathomable talent or luck but as an example of humans exercising the highest level of their intelligence. (Eisner, 1994, p. 156)

Eisner's understanding of the "practical" in education is very comprehensive and stretches beyond teaching to include ways of knowing, program designing, lesson planning, evaluating, and researching. In a recent edited book celebrating Eisner's highly productive career, the editors claim: "No one has been a greater champion of the broad utility of artistic and aesthetic paradigms for educational thought and practice than Elliot Eisner" (Uhrmacher & Matthews, 2005, p. xvii).

We now jump ahead to 1995. This is the date of the publication of *Understanding curriculum: An introduction to the study of historical and contemporary curriculum discourses*, a book we have already cited. This synoptic text provides the first comprehensive, in-depth examination of the arts of the eclectic in curriculum work. The organizing term in this text for the multi-layered, multi-textual exploration is complicated conversation, which is summarized in the last chapter:

> What you now know is that curriculum is a highly symbolic concept. It is what the older generation chooses to tell the younger generation. So understood, curriculum is intensely historical, political, racial, gendered, phenomenological, autobiographical, aesthetic, theological, and international. Curriculum becomes the site on which the generations struggle to define themselves and the world. Curriculum is an extraordinarily complicated conversation. (Pinar, Reynolds, Slattery, & Taubman, 1995, pp. 847–848)

With this statement, the eclectic arts that lie at the heart of disciplined curriculum work are clarified in a coherent and comprehensive way; however, Schwab's linkage of the arts of the eclectic and the arts of the practical through a deliberative artistry needs further reflection and analysis. With respect to Schwab's argument, curriculum work can become disciplined when complicated curriculum conversations turn into sophisticated curriculum deliberations; but how does this occur? The *JCP* is dedicated to exploring this question, fully recognizing that answers to this question require a deep feel for human artistry.

References

Bobbitt, F. (1918). *The curriculum*. New York: Houghton Mifflin.

Eisner, E. (1994). *The educational imagination: On the design and evaluation of school programs* (3rd ed.). New York: Macmillan. (1st ed., published 1979)

Kliebard, H. M. (1997). The rise of scientific curriculum making and its aftermath. In D. J. Flinders & S. J. Thornton (Eds.), *The curriculum studies reader* (pp. 31–44). New York: Routledge. (Original work published 1975)

Marshall, J. D., Sears, J. T., & Schubert, W. H. (2000). *Turning points in curriculum: A contemporary American memoir.* Upper Saddle River, NJ: Merrill/Prentice Hall.

Pinar, W. F. (2004). The synoptic text today. *JCT: An International Journal of Curriculum Studies, 21*(2), 7-22.

Pinar, W. F., Reynolds, W. M., Slattery, P., & Taubman, P. M. (1995). *Understanding curriculum: An introduction to the study of historical and contemporary curriculum discourses.* New York: Peter Lang.

Schwab, J. J. (1969). The practical: A language for curriculum. *School Review, 78,* 1–23.

Schwab, J. J. (2000). The practical: A language for curriculum. Excerpted in J. D. Marshall, J. T. Sears, and W. H. Schubert. Turning points in curriculum: A contemporary American memoir (pp. 95-101). Upper Saddle River, NJ: Merrill/Prentice Hall.

Schwab, J. J. (1971). The practical: Arts of the eclectic. *School Review, 79,* 493–542.

Schwab, J. J. (1973). The practical 3: Translation into curriculum. *School Review, 81,* 501–522.

Schwab, J. J. (1983). The practical 4: Something for curriculum professors to do. *Curriculum Inquiry, 13*(3), 239–265.

Stanley, W. B. (1992). *Curriculum for utopia: Social reconstructionism and critical pedagogy in the postmodern era.* Albany, NY: State University of New York Press.

Tyler, R. W. (1949). *Basic principles of curriculum and instruction.* Chicago: University of Chicago Press.

Uhrmacher, P. B., & Matthews, J. (Eds.). (2005). *Intricate palette: Working the ideas of Elliot Eisner.* Upper Saddle River, NJ: Merrill/Prentice Hall.

Pushing Beyond Social Engineering

The *JCP* is committed to the disciplined understanding and creative enactment of a sophisticated form of educational work that we conceptualize as curriculum-and-pedagogy. We dropped the hyphens in our journal's title, but they are always there in our minds. As editors of the *JCP*, we want you to say "curriculum and pedagogy" without taking a breath—without making any hard and fast distinctions. We want you to recognize that curriculum and pedagogy are deeply embedded in one another. The French language is filled with elisions, which capture the soft boundaries, fluidity and interplay of certain words. We treat curriculum-and-pedagogy as an elided term; and in our last issue, we celebrated Joseph Schwab's essay, *The practical: A language for curriculum* (Schwab, 1969), as a groundbreaking articulation of this professional understanding. Schwab argued that the curriculum field was defined by its eclectic, practical artistry. We further noted the notion of curriculum as a complicated conversation clarified the eclectic artistry in, *Understanding curriculum* (Pinar, Reynolds, Slattery, & Taubman, 1995), while Elliot Eisner's (1994) notion of educational imagination clarified the practical artistry.

We now turn to selected themes that provide further insight into curriculum and pedagogy. For good and bad, education is deeply impacted by policy mandates; and currently, these mandates foster the increased standardization of teaching and learning. This policy trend is based on a "social engineering" logic that is critiqued in William Pinar's essay, *The problem with curriculum and pedagogy*. Since the standardization of education undermines the dynamic interplay between curriculum and pedagogy, educators — including professors in academic settings and teachers in school settings — must work together to responsibly challenge this social engineering resurgence. They must work as visionary public intellectuals and leaders, and this will require the practice of a certain kind of disciplined professional inquiry. Pinar provides insight into how this inquiry must be enacted.

Curriculum workers must proceed in two ways. They must establish an informed critical distance from all overt and covert social engineering applications, and they must inquire into the nature and value of constructive alternatives to engineered learning. Pinar argues that these constructive alternatives must be based on the recognition and affirmation that "study" is the central dynamic of education, and we think you will find his argument both provocative and enlightening. In effect, Pinar is advancing a doubled inquiry logic: the disciplined study of study as learning.

Curriculum and pedagogy involves more than disciplined inquiry. It is a form of sophisticated educational action that requires a deliberative, flexible judgment attuned to contextual contingencies. Thoughtful decisions must be made on how to locate the "wiggle room" (Cuban, 2003) in standardized educational systems and how to enact progressive alternatives. But where do curriculum workers find the necessary room to maneuver? How do they interpret progressive alternatives? And how can and should they act with integrity?

Two of the contributions to Volume 2, Number 1 advanced the journal's mission as well as probed deeper into the concept of social engineering in several important ways. Education and eros are as integrally linked as curriculum and pedagogy. As Pinar discussed in his essay, *The problem with cur-*

riculum and pedagogy this deep connection between education and eros is elucidated by Schwab and by historically significant essayists outside the curriculum field, including Montaigne and Marcuse. Also, Gerda Wever-Rabehl's essay, entitled *Education: The wisdom to live and love*, examines how curriculum workers can educate for citizens who care deeply for other humans and other forms of life, and she celebrates the deep feel for a loving way—a Tao—that lies at the heart of curriculum-and-pedagogical artistry. She drew her inspiration from Eastern philosophies which, interestingly, never fostered the creation of ideologically-based rational systems. This is a relevant point to contemplate in this issue since social engineering through standardization is only "commonsensical" in cultures that support the creation and maintenance of assertive, imperialistic rational systems. In effect, the Tyler Rationale (1949) is a footnote to Descartes' Discourse on Method (1637/1980). As an extrapolation of Cartesian rationality, the Tyler Rationale exudes modernist control and lacks democratic vision. Its narrow pragmatism, decried by Pinar in his essay, dampens the underlying dynamic, pluralistic spirit of curriculum and pedagogy. Social engineering through standardization is an artifact of top-down disciplinary directives, while curriculum and pedagogy is the embodiment of a disciplined openness that enables educators to face down corporatization and other forms of social control while embracing a democratic love of self and others.

References

Cuban, L. (2003). *Why is it so hard to get good schools?* New York: Teachers College Press.

Descartes, R. (1980). *Discourse on method and meditations on first philosophy* (D. A. Cress, Trans.). Indianapolis, IN: Hackett Publishing. (Original work published, 1637)

Eisner, E. (1994). *The educational imagination: On the design and evaluation of school programs* (3rd ed.). New York: Macmillan. (1st ed., published, 1979).

Pinar, W. F., Reynolds, W. M., Slattery, P., & Taubman, P. M. (1995). *Understanding curriculum: An introduction to the study of historical and contemporary curriculum discourses.* New York: Peter Lang.

Schwab, J. J. (1969). The practical: A language for curriculum. *School Review, 78,* 1-23.

Tyler, R. W. (1949). *Basic principles of curriculum and instruction.* Chicago: University of Chicago Press.

Examining Democracy, Spirituality, and Ethics in C&P

In the previous Editors' Introduction (Volume 2, Number 1), we briefly discussed the multidisciplinary, interdisciplinary, and transdisciplinary nature of curriculum and pedagogy in societies with democratic ideals. We noted that progressive educators who are committed to curriculum-based pedagogy hold themselves to a very high professional standard. In their daily decisions about meaningful educational standards, creative program designs and lesson plans, caring teaching-learning transactions, authentic evaluations, and productive work-day structures, they enact a sophisticated deliberative artistry. They challenge the institutional compartmentalization, fragmentation, and standardization that is characteristic of social engineering interventions through holistic envisioning, systemic problem solving, and disciplined reflecting. Simply put, their day-to-day deliberations are imaginative, contextual, multi-layered, nuanced, and ethical.

We noted that this deliberative artistry is informed by the theorizing of Joseph Schwab, Elliot Eisner, and William Pinar, as well as many other curriculum scholars. Educators who practice curriculum-based pedagogy think about the "arts of the practical" and the "arts of the eclectic" (Schwab, 1969/2004 & 1971), about "educational imagination" (Eisner, 1994), and about curriculum as "complicated conversation" (Pinar, 2004). They undertake a personalized, disciplined journey of self-awareness as democratic educators. Pinar characterizes this journey as "currere," which is the infinitive form of curriculum. He writes: "The method of currere reconceptualized curriculum from course objectives to complicated conversation with oneself (as a private intellectual), an ongoing project of self-understanding in which one becomes mobilized for engaged pedagogical action—as a private-and-public intellectual—with others in the social reconstruction of the public sphere" (Pinar, 2004, p. 37). This journey of self-awareness is facilitated by a reflective inquiry that marries a multi-faceted, democratic curriculum inquiry with a continuous reflective practice (Henderson & Gornik, 2006).

All of us in the curriculum and pedagogy community recognize that the enactment of this deliberative artistry on a daily basis is very demanding. Among its many personal and professional challenges, it calls for an understanding of the characteristics of "deep democracy" (Green, 1999), aptly summarized by Kesson (2004): "Deep democracy, or the cultural dimension of formal democracy, requires citizens who are self-reflective, interpersonally engaged, caring, imaginative, inquiring, and communicative" (p. xix). The cultivation of this understanding— formally speaking, the practice of a democratic educational hermeneutics—calls for disciplined spiritual attunement and insight. A recent essay in Cleveland, Ohio's main newspaper, The Plain Dealer, is entitled, *Praying for the demise of religion* (Chalker, 2005). In this article, a United Methodist Church pastor, who has been ministering for 31 years, distinguishes between spirituality and religion:

> God is spirit and thus never captured in a picture, idea, book or creed. Rather, the Holy One is always mysterious, awe inspiring…. Religion, however, is what Satan devises as a way of confusing faithful people. Holy wars, suicide bombings and other religiously motivated killings prove the point…. In these religious times, church organizations are forsaking their initial spiritual impetus and [are] going over to the dark side. (p. 7)

In a similar fashion, the spirit of democratic living is never captured in ideological posturing and scripting. It requires fluid modes of address (Ellsworth, 1997) that are practiced through multiple modes of inquiry (Henderson & Kesson, 2004). This multi-methodology contains an interesting inner/outer discipline. The "complicated conversation" without requires a "complicated conversation" within. Outwardly speaking, democratic freedom is the respectful, humane and fair interplay of diverse, authentic, and caring voices through the practice of responsible autonomy and civility (Greene, 1988; Noddings, 1984). Inwardly speaking, democratic freedom is the embrace of a diversified psychic movement through an open-hearted attunement to the eros—the Tao, or loving way—of democratic pluralism (Garrison, 1997; Slattery, 2006). Goodchild (1996) plays out the moral consequences of such inward/outward interplay: "Supposing thought should function on an ecological plane…. There is no other conclusion that follows from pluralism and multiplicity. …To accept one's ecological finitude in respect of thought and action is to affirm the innocence of existence. It is the one ethical act, above all others, that is needed in our time" (pp. 211, 213).

Where do educators find the spiritual strength to practice this moral-ethical discipline? How do they become attuned to their own "spiritual impetus" for democratic education, and how can the spirit of democratic living inform their professional deliberations? These are pressing questions in this era of manufactured divisiveness, calculated incivility, and religious righteousness—all practiced in the name of "freedom." Here in the United States, we are currently experiencing the emergence of a democratic fascism and a disregard for basic human rights, which can be confusing to those who have faith in democratic freedom. Americans are experiencing

"Satan's work" in a new garb. We think the work from Volume 2, Number 1 provides a timely exploration of how to avoid the snares of evil while embracing democratic morality in the context of curriculum-based pedagogy.

References

Chalker, K. W. (2005, December 12). Praying for the demise of religion. *The Plain Dealer*, Forum, p. 7.

Eisner, E. W. (1994). *The educational imagination: On the design and evaluation of school programs* (3rd ed.). New York: Macmillan. (Original work published 1979)

Ellsworth, E. (1997). *Teaching positions: Difference, pedagogy, and the power of address*. New York: Teachers College Press.

Garrison, J. (1997). *Dewey and eros: Wisdom and desire in the art of teaching*. New York: Teachers College Press.

Goodchild, P. (1996). *Deleuze and Guattari: An introduction to the politics of desire*. Thousand Oaks, CA: Sage Publications.

Green, J. M. (1999). *Deep democracy: Community, diversity, and transformation*. Lanham, MD: Rowman & Littlefield.

Greene, M. (1988). *The dialectic of freedom*. New York: Teachers College Press.

Henderson, J. G., & Gornik, R. (2006). *Transformative curriculum leadership* (3rd ed.). Upper Saddle River, NJ: Merrill/Prentice Hall.

Henderson, J. G., & Kesson, K. R. (2004). *Curriculum wisdom: Educational decisions in democratic societies*. Upper Saddle River, NJ: Merrill/Prentice Hall.

Kesson, K. R. (2004). Introduction: Teaching for a democratic society. In K. R. Kesson (Ed.), *Defending public schools: Teaching for a democratic society* (pp. xvii — xxviii). Westport, CT: Praeger Publishers.

Noddings, N. (1984). *Caring: A feminine approach to ethics and moral education*. Berkeley, CA: University of California Press.

Pinar, W. F. (2004). *What is curriculum theory?* Mahwah, New Jersey: Erlbaum Associates.

Schwab, J. J. (1971). The practical: Arts of the eclectic. *School Review, 79*, 493-542.

Schwab, J. J. (2004). The practical: A language for curriculum. In D. J. Flinders & S. J. Thornton (Eds.), *The curriculum studies reader* (2nd ed., pp. 103-117). New York: RoutledgeFalmer. (Original work published 1969)

Slattery, P. (2006). *Curriculum development in the postmodern era*. (2nd ed.). New York: Routledge.

Committing to Democratic Spaces in C&P

The *JCP* is one of the ongoing publications of the Curriculum and Pedagogy (C&P) Group. This professional association of educators, including both school and university based practitioners/scholars, was formally initiated at the first annual C&P conference in 2000 at the Balcones Conference Center in Marble Fall, Texas. At the sixth annual conference, which was held at Miami University in Oxford, Ohio on October 6-9, 2005, those in attendance participated in a Saturday morning town meeting[1] on the possibility of "Building a Public Disciplinary Community." This is a relevant concern for an important reason. The C&P Group is committed to the study and practice of a critically-informed teaching, called "pedagogy," which is informed by an understanding of curriculum and an understanding of democratic education. In effect, the C&P Group is formally committed to pedagogical artistry informed by a doubled understanding—one linked to an academic heritage called curriculum studies, and one linked to a cultural-historical heritage called democratic living.

If the C&P Group is to evolve into a robust collegial community, all those who actively participate in this association must take on the challenge of engaging in the arts of cultivating this doubled understanding. As Garrison (1997) notes, there is a basic principle underlying human *eros*: we human beings become what we desire! Therefore, what do those of us who attend the annual C&P meeting, and/or those of us who participate in or lend our names to C&P publications, desire? Do we desire to practice a pedagogy that is informed by understanding curriculum and understanding democratic living in education? If not, how do we perceive the C&P Group's and this journal's mission statements? Are these statements just high-minded but, ultimately, meaningless exercises in academic rhetoric? In other words, are these C&P mission statements just "academic?" However, if we do possess the desire to practice a pedagogy that is informed by understanding curriculum and understanding democratic living in education, then our group's formal commitment becomes a personal commitment; and if we share such a personal commitment, then there is a good possibility that we can build a public disciplinary community.

---

[1] As the presiding co-chair of the Curriculum and Pedagogy Council, Donna Adair Breault was responsible for the design and the organization of the Saturday town meeting, while Tom Kelly served as the formal facilitator of the town meeting, which was attended by more than one hundred people.

We cannot proceed with our community-building without clarifying the general parameters of this practical art of understanding—this hermeneutic undertaking—that has just been introduced. In the context of any particular pedagogical practice, how does one understand curriculum, and how does one understand democratic living in education? This is a very complex question requiring much future soul-searching, dialogue, deliberation, and reflection. Though we do not presume to know the answer to this question, we feel there is a way to clarify this hermeneutic challenge; and as we proceed with our explanation, we invite further input and alternative insights.

We begin with the work in curriculum studies scholarship in *Understanding curriculum* (Pinar, Reynolds, Slattery, & Taubman, 1995) where curriculum understanding emerges out of an "extraordinarily complicated conversation" containing "historical, political, racial, gendered, phenomenological, autobiographical, aesthetic, theological, and international" subtexts. (pp. 847–848). Pinar et al. are arguing that educators must become conversant in a wide range of contemporary curriculum discourses; otherwise, they cannot properly understand the curriculum. In effect, they are making a particular disciplinary point: educators must practice the discipline of a multi-textual and curricular "complicated conversation" if they desire to understand curriculum.

With reference to the question of understanding democratic living in education, educators confront the fact that, as philosophers duly note, democracy is an "essentially contested concept." Democracy has diverse interpretations, many of them emotionally charged and ideologically scripted. Consequently, the question of how to live democratically is, essentially, ambiguous. From a more libertarian point of view, does it mean that "individuals can maximally pursue their self-defining activities" (Hoffert, 2001, p. 34); or from a more egalitarian perspective, does it mean that members of a particular society have a collective responsibility, enacted through the auspices of their democratically elected representatives, to ensure just, equitable and humane social conditions?

John Dewey enters this interpretive thicket from a particular point of view. His work focuses on the quality of experience that is gradually realized through its democratization. In advancing his interpretation of democratic living, he asks the following question: "Can we find any reason that does not ultimately come down to the belief that democratic social arrangements promote a better quality of human experience, one which is more widely accessible and enjoyed, than do non-democratic and anti-democratic forms of social life?" (Dewey, 1938/1998, p. 25). Dewey is arguing that those who seek to understand quality human experience must consider its democratization; and in fact, Dewey considered using the terms "transaction" and "culture" to better communicate his particular interpretation of quality "experience" near the end of his long and productive career (Jackson, 2002; Jay, 2005).

In effect, Dewey understood democratic living as a continuous and deepening democratization of experience. Furthermore, in this hermeneutic context, he took the following position on the meaning of freedom:

> Genuine freedom in short, is intellectual; it rests in the trained *power of thought*, in an ability to "turn things over," to look at matters deliberately, to judge whether the amount and kind of evidence requisite for decision is at hand, and if not, to tell where and how to seek such evidence. If a man's [or woman's] actions are not guided by thoughtful conclusions, then they are guided by inconsiderate impulse, unbalanced appetite, caprice, or the circumstances of the moment. To cultivate unhindered, unreflective external activity is to foster enslavement, for it leaves the person at the mercy of appetite, sense, and circumstance. (Dewey 1910/1978, p. 232)

Let us now briefly consider the implications of Dewey's view of "democratic freedom" for disciplined curriculum-based pedagogy. The enactment of democratic living in education requires the practice of professional deliberative judgments that are directed toward the facilitation of students' deliberative judgments. Otherwise, the curriculum and pedagogical work, and the student learning that emerges out of this work, lacks disciplinary focus.

The deliberative judgment that Dewey is advancing is, necessarily, embedded in a multi-modal inquiry. Martin Jay's (2005) *Songs of experience* provides insight into why this is so. In his book, Jay presents a wide range of interpretations of human experience that have been carefully crafted and articulated in the European-American historical context over the past 2,000 years. Borrowing the title of his book from one of William Blake's poem cycles, he organizes his discussion into the following categories: epistemological, religious, aesthetic, political, historical, pragmatic, critical and poststructural; and he argues that human experience is best understood in "heterodox ways" (p. 8). He takes the position that human experience cannot be understood through one particular modality. He explains:

> The dangers of compartmentalizing experience can already be sighted as early as the Romantics and is evident in idealists like Hegel. It was perhaps only in the twentieth century that the chorus grew to encompass thinkers from many, often very different, traditions— philosophical as well as political. Hoping to recapture a more robust, intense, and all-encompassing notion of experience—whether it be called "authentic" or "essential" or "pure" or "inner"—they sought to reverse the process of

differentiation. Often betraying a sense of nostalgia for what had pur-
portedly been lost by modalization, they hoped to make whole what had
been torn asunder, reinvigorating a common life world that had relin-
quished its coherent meaning with the development of subcultures of expertise. Although an important difference separated those who thought
the problem was inherently conceptual or philosophical—all that was
needed, they contended, was a better grasp of what experience always
already is—from those who insisted the real cause of the loss was a crisis
in the larger social or cultural world as a whole, both decried differentiation as a process to be reversed. And they did so in that rhapsodic tone
so often accompanying evocations of the word "experience," a tone al-
lowing us to borrow William Blake's title for our own. (pp. 262–263)

Jay is arguing that those who seek to understand human experience must
reject the modernist heritage of "modalization." They must avoid a narrow
interpretive compartmentalization and expertise as they proceed with their
hermeneutic undertaking, and the design of his book serves as a model on
how they must proceed. In effect, Jay is making a particular disciplinary
point that is parallel with Pinar et al.'s disciplinary point. Jay is arguing that
individuals—including, of course, all educators— must engage in the discipline of multi-modal inquiry if they desire to understand experience. Jay's
disciplinary perspective is applied to the practice of curriculum-based pedagogical judgment in Henderson and Kesson's *Curriculum wisdom*. They write:

Curriculum wisdom…is a quality of consciousness that moves fluidly
and freely between the sacred and the profane, or the world of the gods
and the world of mortals. The process of "envisioning" involves insight
and imagination—the world of the gods. The process of "enacting" involves social criticism and informed practicality—the world of mortals.
Envisioning and enacting are incomplete without each other. When in
play together, they constitute "the Tao of curriculum wisdom." To meet
this curriculum wisdom challenge of envisioning and enacting, we have
identified seven inquiry domains… These seven modes of inquiry are:
techne (craft reflection), *poesis* (soulful attunement to the creative process), praxis (critical inquiry); *dialogos* (multiperspectival inquiry); *phrone-
sis* (practical, deliberative wisdom), polis (public moral inquiry); and
theoria (contemplative wisdom). (Henderson & Kesson, 2004, p. 47)

After introducing the details of their multi-modal inquiry "map" for professional judgment, Henderson and Kesson invite readers to identify a specific
problem and then ask themselves questions that flow from each mode of
inquiry. As part of this disciplined questioning, the readers are advised to
seek out individuals who may possess a deeper insight into a particular

mode of inquiry so as "to see the strength in their perspective and the flaws in your own" (Henderson & Kesson, 2004, p. 63).

We can now advance a hermeneutic blueprint for the professional challenge of building a public disciplinary community. Such an effort would be guided by the following methodological principles:

1. It would be embedded in a "complicated conversation" involving a broad and diverse set of curriculum discourses. Those who engage in the collegial dialogue would be conversant with, and draw upon, contemporary curriculum studies.

2. There would be a focus on the democratization of educational experience, and this discussion would allow for insights from diverse views on the meaning of democratic living. Particular political ideologies would inform, but not dominate, the art of understanding; and care would be taken to stay focused on the multi-modal complexities of experience.

3. It would be guided by a multi-modal inquiry into democratic educational experience. No one mode of inquiry—political, aesthetic, spiritual, and so on—would command attention; and care would be taken to ensure a broad horizon of questioning.

4. There would be a discussion about the nature of curriculum-based pedagogical judgment. There would be a focus on how deliberative judgment should be conceptualized and practiced, particularly with reference to the democratization of teaching-learning transactions.

5. There would be a discussion about how to impact the public imaginary. How can the emerging C&P community identify and communicate with selected publics on the meaning of "democratic freedom" in education in an era dominated by capitalistic consumerism, ideological tribalism, scientific management and postmodern diffusion?

References

Dewey, J. (1978). How we think. In J. A. Boydston (Ed.), *John Dewey: The middle works, 1899–1924*. (Vol. 6: 1910–1911, pp. 177–356). Carbondale, IL: Southern Illinois University Press. (Original work published 1910)

Dewey, J. 1998. *Experience and education*. West Lafayette, IN: Kappa Delta Pi. (Original work published 1938)

Garrison, J. (1997). *Dewey and eros: Wisdom and desire in the art of teaching.* New York: Teachers College Press.

Henderson, J. G., & Kesson, K. R. (2004). *Curriculum wisdom: Educational decisions in democratic societies.* Upper Saddle River, NJ: Merrill/Prentice Hall.

Hoffert, R. W. (2001). Education in a political democracy. In R. Soder, J. I. Goodlad, & T. J. McMannon (Eds.), *Developing democratic character in the young* (pp. 26–44). San Francisco, CA: Jossey-Bass.

Jackson, P. W. (2002). *John Dewey and the philosopher's task.* New York: Teachers College Press.

Jay, M. (2005). *Songs of experience: Modern American and European variations on a universal theme.* Berkeley, CA: University of California Press.

Pinar, W. F., Reynolds, W. M., Slattery, P., & Taubman, P. M. (1995). *Understanding curriculum: An introduction to the study of historical and contemporary curriculum discourses.* New York: Peter Lang.

Supporting the Process of Becoming/Knowing/Doing

In the Editors' Introduction in *JCP* Summer 2006 issue (Volume 3, Number 1), we advanced a blueprint for building a public disciplinary community committed to enacting the Curriculum & Pedagogy (C&P) mission statement that is published in each issue of this journal. We made five points. The community building efforts will need to be: (1) embedded in a "complicated conversation" (Pinar, 2004) involving a broad and diverse set of contemporary curriculum discourses, (2) focused on the democratization of educational experience, (3) guided by multi-modal inquiry, (4) interested in deliberative pedagogical judgment, and (5) concerned about impacting the public imaginary. We recognize that this five-part agenda is personally and professionally challenging, but we are comforted by the fact that most, if not all, educators who attend the annual C&P conferences and/or read C&P publications understand the importance of this type of community building. We must constantly challenge ourselves to examine our mission and find ways to improve our conferences and publications. We feel optimistic about the future of the C&P community, and we want to put forward a proposal that, we feel, has enormous implications for actualizing the C&P mission and, assuming that it would be enacted beyond the immediate C&P circle, for realizing the full potential of educational artistry in societies with democratic ideals.

Our proposal is based on two historically significant shifts in human consciousness. The first shift occurred in Ancient Greek times and is documented by Pierre Hadot in his book, *Philosophy as a way of life* (1995). In this book, Hadot chronicles how a tradition of "spiritual discipline," embedded in different philosophical schools of thought (Platonic, Aristotelian, Stoic, Epicurean, Cynic, Pyrrhonic, and so on), was invented and practiced. Though the philosophical projects of the diverse schools were quite distinctive, they shared the recognition that a philosophical way of life involved a disciplined integration of a way of being, a way of knowing, and a way of doing. People who engaged in this discipline were called "philosophers," that is, people who possessed a love of wisdom. They were "atopos," that is, "unclassifiable" (Hadot, 1995, p. 57). In the spirit of Maxine Greene's *Teacher as stranger* (1973), they did not fit into any identifiable socio-cultural categories. Hadot (1995) explains:

> What makes [Socrates and philosophers like him] atopos is precisely the fact that he (sic) is a "philosopher" in the etymological sense of the word; that is, he is in love with wisdom. For wisdom, says Diotima in Plato's Symposium, is not a human state, it is a state of perfection of being and knowledge that can only be divine. It is the love of this wisdom, which is foreign to the world, that makes the philosopher a stranger in it. [The philosopher] knows that normal natural state of [humanity]…should be wisdom, for wisdom is nothing more than the vision of the…cosmos as it is in the light of reason, and wisdom is also nothing more than the mode of being and living that should correspond to this vision. (pp. 57-58)

In the context of this tradition of spiritual discipline, Socrates, perhaps, best represents both the comprehensiveness and the humility of this love of wisdom (Hadot, 2002). He embodied the integrity of integrating being, thinking and doing; and he did so fully recognizing that he could never be wise. Socrates understood that since only "God" (or the "gods") could be wise, the best he could do would be to practice a love of wisdom through disciplined inquiry, dialogue, and self-examination. The fact that Plato lost touch with this sense of humility and became an advocate for a particular "idealist" theology need not reflect poorly on Socrates' philosophical integrity (Garrison, 1997). After all, how fair is it to blame the teacher for the student's errant ways?

The second shift in consciousness is deeply connected to the ancient Greek heritage of "spiritual discipline;" and it is, in part, understandable in light of Plato's "idealist" theology which, of course, deeply influenced the direction of Western philosophy. Beginning in the 1870's, a group of philosophers in Europe and the United States turned to human "experience" as the critical focus for their work. They did so because they were dissatisfied with the philosophical systems of their day. Kloppenberg (1986) elaborates:

> The search for alternatives to the idealist and naturalist philosophies dominant in the mid-nineteenth century began in the 1870's and reached fruition during the next three decades. The thinkers who made the most important contributions to this quest for a via media were Wilhelm Dilthey, Thomas Hill Green, Henry Sidgwick, Alfred Fouilléée, William James, and John Dewey. These mavericks insisted that ideas emerge from, and must be validated in, neither language nor logic but life. Theirs was a profoundly historical sensibility, imbued with the belief that meaning is woven into the fiber of experience, that becoming rather than being is the mode of human life, and that people make rather than find their values. I will call this cluster of ideas the radical theory of knowledge, radical because it cut to the core of attempts to find an Archimedean point for epistemology and substituted an acceptance of contingency for the standard quest for certainty. (pp. 3-4)

As summarized by Kloppenberg, this group of philosophers reflected the Socratic disposition to be "lovers of wisdom." They embraced the "multiverse" nature of experience and rejected attempts to reduce this complexity to "true" belief systems or "valid" empirical methodologies (Kloppenberg, 1986, p. 61). Rejecting attempts to establish specific theological and/or empirical systems, they affirmed and celebrated the freedom that lies at the heart of meaningful human experience:

> The partisans of an extended empiricism argued that science and theology assume equally strict rules of causality. Within the realm of physical sciences, uncaused or "free" events cannot occur; within the Judeo-Christian tradition, there is likewise room for only one first cause or "unmoved mover." Lived experience, however, in its prereflective immediacy, does not conform to either of these models. We are conscious of the ability to select, to choose among options, and we are further aware that by acting on our decisions we effect change. We experience, in short, the distinct feeling of freedom. (Kloppenberg, 1986, pp. 79-80)

This focus on the "freedom" that is deeply embedded in lived experience results in an important shift in consciousness. The ancient Greek spiritual discipline of being/knowing/doing is reconstructed as a democratic becoming/knowing/doing. This transformation is vividly captured in a question posed by John Dewey in his Experience and Education, which we quoted in the last issue: "Can we find any reason that does not ultimately come down to the belief that democratic social arrangements promote a better quality of human experience, one which is more widely accessible and enjoyed, than do non-democratic and anti-democratic forms of social life?" (Dewey, 1938/1998, p. 25). In effect, Dewey is arguing that becoming "democratic" is the actualization of "quality" experience. This means that people must challenge themselves, in very specific, here-and-now ways, to "walk the talk" of their democratic ideals. They must strive to embody democratic being, knowing, and doing, and they must recognize that this striving requires a disciplined becoming. From the standpoint of education, "curriculum" must necessarily be interpreted as a particular "currere"—as a journey of democratic understanding conducted in the context of each teacher's subject matter responsibilities.

But what does it mean to undertake a journey of "democratic understanding" through educational "experience," particularly in our current historical context with its deeply embedded structures of standardized surveillance? What is the difference between standardized and democratic experience? How do we interpret "democratic" becoming, knowing, and doing; how do we practice the necessary "spiritual" discipline; and which educators are drawn to such a life? These are crucial, critical questions— "critical" with reference to its etymological source as a "pivotal turning point" in the "health" of the patient (Ayto, 1990)—that serve as the basis for our proposal.

We propose that collegial inquiry into "democratic experience in education" needs to become a central feature of our annual C&P conference. This collaborative work, which is informed by Pinar's (2005) insights into the study of curriculum, would be practiced through specific activities that explore the "spiritual discipline" underlying the journal's mission statement. How exactly is the C&P mission embodied daily in educational activities? What is the integral relationship between "democratic" becoming, knowing, and doing? Are we practicing a love of wisdom through disciplined inquiry, dialogue and self-examination, or are we falling into ideological and epistemological traps? Are we creating epistemological curriculum spaces where experience and justice can flourish? Are we staying focused on the here-and-now of experience; or like superficial politicians, are we simply mouthing platitudes and exercising empty rhetoric? What is the integrity of our "C&P" work, and how is this acknowledged and celebrated at our annual meetings? In what sense does our disciplined, holistic lifestyle make us atopos, "strange;" and how do we support one another in negotiating this strangeness under current modern and emerging postmodern conditions? Finally, as we cultivate our critical awareness of "democratic experience in education," how do we function as transformative leaders who invite and inspire others to elevate their critical awareness?

We leave deliberating over the details of our proposal to specific future forums. However, we conclude by acknowledging that we are addressing a pressing historical problem. In his 1938 essay, Dewey challenges "progressive" educators to critically study the democratization of "experience" in education for purposes of better understanding their avowed educational philosophy:

> I take it that the fundamental unity of the newer philosophy is found in the idea that there is an intimate and necessary relation between the processes of actual experience and education. If this be true, then a positive and constructive development of its own basic idea depends upon having a correct idea of experience. When external control is rejected, the problem becomes that of finding the factors of control that are inherent within experience. ...It is not too much to say that an educational philosophy which professes to be based on the idea of freedom may become as dogmatic as ever was the traditional education which is reacted against. For any theory and set of practices is dogmatic which is not based upon critical examination of its own underlying principles. (Dewey, 1938/1998, pp. 7-10)

How well have we "progressive" educators responded to the challenge Dewey articulates? Dewey argued for the disciplined "critical examination" of educational experience sixty-nine years ago. How would C&P educators, and more broadly all contemporary educators, respond to Dewey's challenge in 2007? How exactly are we critically inquiring into the relationship between education and experience in societies with democratic ideals, and how do we embody this critical awareness through a "spiritual" discipline? Collegially exploring these questions could further focus our C&P community-building efforts.

References

Ayto, J. (1990). *Dictionary of word origins*. New York: Arcade Publishing/Little, Brown and Company.

Dewey, J. (1998). *Experience and education*. West Lafayette, IN: Kappa Delta Pi. (Original work published 1938)

Garrison, J. (1997). *Dewey and eros: Wisdom and desire in the art of teaching*. New York: Teachers College Press.

Greene, M. (1973). *Teacher as stranger: Educational philosophy for the modern age*. Belmont, CA: Wadsworth.

Hadot, P. (1995). *Philosophy as a way of life: Spiritual exercises from Socrates to Foucault* (M. Chase, Trans.). Malden, MA: Blackwell Publishing.

Hadot, P. (2002). *What is ancient philosophy?* (M. Chase, Trans.). Cambridge, MA: Belknap Press/Harvard University Press.

Kloppenberg, J. T. (1986). *Uncertain victory: Social democracy and progressivism in European and American thought, 1870-1920*. New York: Oxford University Press.

Pinar, W. F. (2004). *What is curriculum theory?* Mahwah, NJ: Lawrence Erlbaum Associates.

Pinar, W. F. (2005). The problem with curriculum and pedagogy. *Journal of Curriculum and Pedagogy, 2*(1), 67-82.

Discussing Ethical Challenges in Curriculum and Pedagogy

In our role as co-editors of the *JCP*, we sought to advance and understand the general parameters of "curriculum and pedagogy" community building, and we have been noting that our interpretation draws on our journal's mission statement and on the Curriculum and Pedagogy Group's mission statement. We summarized our argument in the last issue:

> The [Curriculum and Pedagogy (C&P)] community building efforts will need to be: (1) embedded in a "complicated conversation" (Pinar, 2004) involving a broad and diverse set of contemporary curriculum discourses, (2) focused on the democratization of educational experience, (3) guided by multi-modal inquiry, (4) interested in deliberative pedagogical judgment, and (5) concerned about impacting the public imaginary. We recognize that this five-part agenda is personally and professionally challenging, but we are comforted by the fact that most, if not all, educators who attend the annual C&P conferences and/or read C&P publications understand the importance of this type of community building. (Henderson & Slattery, 2006, p. 1)

For the focus of the Volume 4, Number 1 issue we wanted to highlight the ethical inquiries underlying this agenda. This part of our argument draws on the insights of three Continental philosophers and is based on a particular distillation of the *JCP* and C&P group mission statements. We begin with the mission statements.

Two key interrelated principles can be discerned from these two documents. First, our work is committed to the synergy between curriculum study and pedagogical enactment. We, therefore, challenge the theory-practice binary whenever and however it emerges. We work hard to understand what Pinar (2007) characterizes as the "vertical" and "horizontal" dimensions of curriculum studies[2]; and we explore creative ways to integrate our curriculum studies into all aspects of our curriculum practices, including goal setting, designing, planning, teaching, evaluating, and organizing (Henderson & Gornik, 2007).

The second principle builds on the first: our disciplined efforts at study-practice synergy are situated in the *democratization* of educational experience. We are committed to studying and realizing a "deep democracy" (Green, 1999) in education; and we recognize that, due to current historical circumstances, this is more a matter of becoming than being. We humbly acknowledge how little we understand democratic experience in all of its complexities and mysteries, so we openly embrace the necessary individual and collegial disciplined inquiry. We appreciate that we are taking a particular normative position concerning educational practices, succinctly captured in Dewey's (1938/1998) pragmatic question: "Can we find any reason that does not ultimately come down to the belief that democratic social arrangements promote a better quality of human experience, one which is more widely accessible and enjoyed, than do non-democratic and anti-democratic forms of social life?" (p. 25).

We will shortly present a set of ethical inquiries based on these two interrelated principles, but first we need to introduce several sophisticated concepts that are drawn from the work of three Continental philosophers. Deleuze and Guattari (1980/1987) explore the vital relationship between a 'plane of immanence' and its 'lines of flight.' The plane of immanence is the postmodern equivalent of an educational platform. It is a metaphor conveying a sense of being grounded in infinite space. Picture a plane in space. How many planes can you imagine? There are limitless possibilities (Badiou, 2005). The image of boundless 'planes-in-space' conveys an appreciation that any particular normative position can always be challenged from a different position — from a different plane of being.

---

[2] Pinar (2007) writes: "The first of the disciplinary structures is verticality, by which I mean the intellectual history of the discipline. What ideas formulated in earlier eras inform my own?... The second disciplinary structure...is horizontality: analyses of its present circumstances. Horizontality refers not only to the field's present set of intellectual circumstances -as, for instance, I attempted to portray in my 1978 the state-of-the-field address (Pinar, 1994)- but as well the social and political milieu which influences and, all too often, structures this set" (pp. 3, 5).

A plane of immanence also conveys the sense of being pregnant with possibilities. In Dewey's (1938/1998) language, such a plane has rich "educative" potential. It is generative. Growth is close at hand, proximate, momentary, and immediate. A plane of immanence encourages and provokes lift-offs, creative leaps, and plays of interpretations. It can be compared to a bouncy trampoline that invites multiple lines of flight. With reference to the two interrelated principles, the growth possibilities inherent in a study-practice synergy situated in the democratic here-and-now are enormous. There is much promise for engaging in a diversified but disciplined meaning making through multi-modal inquiries.[3]

This sense of disciplined openness is further clarified by another key concept advanced by Badiou—the notion of 'ethical fidelity.' The creation of the *JCP*, and the C&P Group's mission statements are key events in our community building efforts; therefore, our explication of a study-practice synergy situated in the democratic here-and-now can be characterized as a 'supplement' to these two key professional events. Badiou (2001) notes that a supplement to an event is an expression of ethical fidelity, which challenges individuals "to invent a new way of being and acting in the situation." (p. 42) He elaborates:

> Essentially, a truth is the material course traced, within the situation, by the eventral supplementation. It is thus an *immanent break*. 'Immanent' because a truth proceeds *in* the situation, and nowhere else—there is no heaven of truths....I call 'subject' the bearer...of a fidelity, the one who bears a process of truth. The subject, therefore, in no way pre-exists the process. He [or she] is absolutely nonexistent in the situation 'before' the event. We might say that the process of truth *induces* a subject. (pp. 42-43, author's emphasis)

There are two key points associated with Badiou's notion of ethical fidelity. There is the sense of being faithful to underlying commitments. In the case of this journal and its professional association, this poses the question of our enduring commitment to the two mission statements. Do we perceive these two statements as perfunctory exercises merely to be stored in long-forgotten files, or do we see them as documents meant to be lived? This question brings us to Badiou's second point. The mission statements call forth a 'subjectivity' that is immanent within the C&P advocacy and that may require a profound break with our professional pasts. In effect, to play

---

[3] For a further discussion of the general parameters of this multi-modal inquiry, see Henderson and Slattery, 2006.

out the ethical fidelity of the mission statements is not only to engage in lines of flight that emerge from a particular plane of imminence but to, possibly, undertake news ways of being and acting that embody a new professional identity. Are we up to the challenge?

We are optimistic that the C&P com-munity is ready for this challenge. We are confident that we can practice the necessary fidelity. In the spirit of Dewey's (1930/1999) call for a "new individualism," we acknowledge that our mission statements are a potential call for a "new professionalism." A study-practice synergy situated in the democratic here-and-now is a very complicated venture involving visionary imagination, soul-searching, and pragmatic artistry. We have to envision new ways of practicing and then seek to integrate our imaginings into our actions.

The set of ethical inquiries that we present below are offered in the spirit of advancing our imaginations and practices in ways that are compatible with the plane of immanence we are advancing. Consistent with the idea of multiple lines of flight, we frame these ethical inquiries in broad terms and invite readers to fill in the inquiry details consistent with their current and evolving understanding of study-practice synergy situated in the democratic here-and-now. We believe that the ethical inquiries apply to all C&P activities, including the work in this journal, the deliberations of the C&P Council, and the practices at the annual conference with its proceedings. The questions are asked in the present tense to convey a sense of immediacy and emergence:

1. Is a curriculum and pedagogy synergy apparent in the activity? If so, how is it being manifested? If not, how is curriculum study being kept separate from the pedagogical practice, or vice versa?

2. With reference to a specific activity, are curriculum theorists and school-based practitioners invited to interact with one another? If so, how is this being done? If not, how is the theory-practice interaction being inhibited, suppressed, or otherwise disallowed and/or ignored?

3. Does the particular synergistic activity embody a democratic quality? If so, how exactly do you perceive this quality? If not, how would you characterize the activity as either being consciously and/or unconsciously undemocratic? What are your criteria for making such affirming and/or critical judgments?

4. Does the particular synergistic activity convey a sense of democratic becoming? If so, how is this being manifested? If not, why do you think this growth is not occurring? Again, what are your criteria for making such affirming and/or critical judgments?

5. With reference to a specific activity, what concrete interventions might be made to foreground and strengthen the democratic nature of the resulting experiences? To this end, what key challenges, dilemmas, tensions, and/or paradoxes might need to be acknowledged, addressed and, perhaps, reconciled?

We present these categories of questions as a way of highlighting the personal and professional significance of our journal's and the Curriculum and Pedagogy Group's mission statements. We do not want these mission statements to be duly noted and then tacitly ignored. We feel it is time to move forward with our collegial commitments, and we invite a broad-based discussion of these ethical inquiries. We recognize that we are undertaking a professional endeavor that has no historical precedent in the educational field.[4]

References

Badiou, A. (2001). *Ethics: An essay on the understanding of evil* (P. Hallward, Trans.). London: Verso.

Badiou, A. (2005). *Infinite thought: Truth and the return to philosophy* (O. Feltham and J. Clemens, Trans. & Eds.). London: Continuum.

Deleuze, G., & Guattari, F. (1987). *A thousand plateaus: Capitalism and schizophrenia* (B. Massumi, Trans.). Minneapolis: University of Minnesota Press. (Original work published 1980)

Dewey, J. (1998). *Experience and education*. West Lafayette, IN: Kappa Delta Pi. (Original work published 1938)

Dewey, J. (1999). *Individualism old and new*. Amherst, NY: Prometheus Books. (Original work published 1930)

Green, J. M. (1999). *Deep democracy: Community, diversity, and transformation*. Lanham, MD: Rowman & Littlefield.

Henderson, J. G., & Gornik, R. (2007). *Transformative curriculum leadership* (3rd ed.). Upper Saddle River, NJ: Merrill/Prentice Hall.

Henderson, J. G., & Slattery, P. (2006). Epistemological challenges and the process of becoming. *Journal of Curriculum and Pedagogy, 3*(2), 1-9.

---

[4] We wish to acknowledge Tom Kelly's key role as a 'critical friend' in clarifying and composing this ethical call.

Pinar, W. F. (2004). *What is curriculum theory?* Mahwah, NJ: Lawrence Erlbaum Associates.

Pinar, W. F. (2007). *Disciplinarity and the intellectual advancement of U.S. curriculum studies: The canon project.* Paper presented at the annual conference of the Association for the Advancement of Curriculum Studies. Chicago, IL.

Understanding Curriculum Leadership

Programs and courses have been developed and approved in "Curriculum Leadership" in both of our universities in recent years. We are also aware of burgeoning program development in "Curriculum Leadership" at other universities, and there seems to be growing interest in the intersection of curriculum, pedagogy, and school leadership. In our books we have advanced a philosophy of *Transformative curriculum leadership* (Henderson & Hawthorne, 1995), *Curriculum wisdom* (Henderson & Kesson, 2004), *Ethics and the foundations of education* (Slattery & Rapp, 2003), and *Curriculum development in the postmodern era* (Slattery, 2006). Patrick has held joint appointments in both Curriculum & Instruction departments and Educational Administration & Human Resource departments throughout his career. Jim has worked in departments that include leadership and curriculum studies. While we strongly support and advance concepts of curriculum leadership from various perspectives, we are concerned about the emphasis on administrative training and test data management in some recent curriculum leadership models. One vision of curriculum leadership emphasizes exclusively the advancement of accountability narratives and No Child Left Behind ideologies for improved test scores. The narrowing of space for understanding curriculum and investigating progressive social and cultural experiences for growth in the spirit of John Dewey (1938) and others is disconcerting.

We are familiar with a large US school administration certification program where the majority of professors are curriculum theorists; we are also familiar with a large program in curriculum leadership certification in a major US university where the professors are almost exclusively quantitative researchers in educational administration. The curriculum theory professors in the Educational Administration program are affiliated with AERA Divisions B and G, the Curriculum and Pedagogy Conference, and Professors of Curriculum. The educational administration professors in the Curriculum Leadership program are affiliated with AERA Divisions A and K, The University Council for Educational Administration (UCEA), and the American Educational Research Journal (AERJ). Of course, there is some overlap in both groups (but not much). It is very interesting for us to observe the ironic juxtaposition of curriculum and pedagogy scholars leading educational leadership certification programs and educational leadership scholars directing curriculum and pedagogy certification programs. What is going on here? Is this phenomenon more widespread than the two anecdotal examples we are familiar with?

Five articles from the Volume 4, Number 2 issue of *JCP* begin to address these questions in ways that will advance a "complicated conversation" (Pinar, 2004) about curriculum leadership. In, *Horizonal leadership: Seeing afresh the face of the other in educational leadership practices* Louise Anderson Allen and Nancy J. Brooks suggested a response to recent calls for the creation of future leaders who are wise, as opposed to simply knowledgeable. They proposed that educational leadership programs fall short in this area. Operating out of an obsolete standardized management paradigm, such programs increase structures of surveillance, such as curriculum "monitoring," that are more suited for teaching leaders what to think than how to think. Peter Maas Taubman's article about accountability entitled, *The tie that binds: Learning and teaching in the new educational order* was framed with a speech by Diane Ravich that was about the assault on public education in the US. Taubman contended that it is interesting to contrast Ravitch's speech with the response of mainstream educators and the educational establishment. Taubman concluded that Ravitch should have foreseen the nightmare resulting from the neo-liberal and neo-conservative assault on education. Jennifer Hauver James' article, *Autobiographical inquiry, teacher education and (the possibility of) social justice* investigated the repeated call for self-examination of teachers as a means of achieving greater social justice in education. The notion that having greater consciousness of the spaces we inhabit and our relation to others, James ponders, may lead us to act more justly in the world and more compassionate in teaching. Susan Jean Mayer's piece, *The ideal as real: John Dewey and the social construction of moral coherence* turned to Dewey's book *A common faith* and contended that although he did not believe in a knowing God, he believed in moral truth and in a human propensity to judge action relative to an emergent moral sensibility. Mayer investigated the conditions and means that Dewey found essential to the social construction of moral coherence and focuses on the relationship Dewey envisioned between the aesthetic and scientific dimensions of human experience. Lastly, Youngjoo Kim's article, *Toward pedagogy that empowers growth: Reflection on a lesson that turned me away from learning* represented an application of the principles of leadership, aesthetic experience, and wisdom that have been discussed in the other essays. Kim contended that the curriculum experience teachers create can help their students extend their limits and reach beyond their self-perceived boundaries.

References

Dewey, J. (1938). *Experience and education*. New York: Macmillan.

Henderson, J. G., & Kesson, K. R. (2004). *Curriculum wisdom: Educational decisions in democratic societies*. Upper Saddle River, NJ: Merrill/Prentice Hall.

Henderson, J. G., & Hawthone, R. D. (1995). *Transformative curriculum leadership*. New York: MacMillan.

Pinar, W. F. (2004). *What is curriculum theory?* Mahwah, NJ: Lawrence Erlbaum Associates.

Slattery, P. (2006). *Curriculum development in the postmodern era* (2nd ed.). New York: Routledge.

Slattery, P., & Rapp, D. (2003). *Ethics and the foundations of education: Teaching convictions in a postmodern world*. Boston: Allyn and Bacon.

Advancing Three Disciplinary Dimensions of Curriculum-Based Pedagogy

In the Editors' Introduction for the Winter, 2007 issue of *JCP* (Volume 4, Number 2), we highlighted the curriculum leadership implications of our "Curriculum and Pedagogy" (C&P) mission. In succinct terms, this mission can be articulated as understanding, enacting, and embodying the synergistic relationship between curriculum studies and pedagogical artistry. Since the very first issue of this journal, we have been working to unpack and explain the subtleties and parameters of this very professional and visionary end-in-view in our Editors' Introductions; and we invite readers of this journal to review the many points we have made since the initial Summer, 2004 issue (Volume 1, Number 1).

In our Editors' Introduction for this issue (Volume 5, Number 1) we wanted to highlight a potentially powerful leadership tool associated with our C&P mission and to describe one success story associated with the use of this tool. With reference to the C&P mission, we identified at least three key disciplinary dimensions underlying curriculum-based pedagogy. Before introducing these three dimensions, we need to clarify our understanding of "professional discipline." We are referring to a discipline that comes from within each person as a result of their professional calling and intentions. Such a discipline is both generative and generous in the spirit of Maxine Greene's (1988) celebration of her "positive" freedom:

> This book arises out of a lifetime's preoccupation with quest, with pursuit. On the one hand, the quest has been deeply personal: that of a woman striving to affirm the feminine as wife, mother, and friend, while reaching, always reaching, beyond the limits imposed by the obligations of a woman's life. On the other hand, it has been in some sense deeply public as well: that of a person struggling to connect the undertaking of education, which she has been so long involved, to the making and re-making of a public space, a space of dialogue and possibility. (p. xi)

Our sense of discipline-from-within is informed by van Manen's (1991) discussion of "pedagogical intent" and Kreisberg's (1992) analysis of "power-with" relations in education. Standing in contrast to this understanding of the use of "power" would be the various power-over practices with their hierarchical structures and strategies, as examined by Foucault (1980) and many other "postmodern" critical theorists.[5] Also standing in contrast to our understanding of discipline-from-within are the various structural interpretations of the academic disciplines, perhaps most significantly the "structures-of-disciplines" movement in curriculum studies during the late 1950's and early 1960's (Ford & Pugno, 1964). In sum, our understanding of professional discipline is informed by postmodern and poststructural critiques.

In this spirit, we celebrate the **disciplined openness** underlying Elliot Eisner's (1994) notion of "productive idiosyncrasy." Uhrmacher and Matthews (2005) provide a concise summary of Eisner's concept:

> During an era obsessed with issues of conformity and standardization, Eisner follows a different path. Influenced by the work of Sir Herbert Read, Eisner argues that education should foster productive *idiosyncrasy* among students, rather than mold all to standard uniformity. In short, he is interested in helping children learn to use their senses to achieve greater degrees of perceptive and expressive differentiation, so that they may formulate concepts and represent them through a variety of forms. (p. 6, authors' emphasis)

---

[5] For a concise, insightful discussion of various interpretations of "power" in research discourse-practices, see Cherryholmes' (1988) footnote #1 on pp. 191-194.

As advocates of an internal C&P "disciplinarity" (Pinar, 2007), we encourage, nurture, honor and applaud diversified "lines of flight" (Deleuze & Guattari, 1980/1987). We invite and affirm multiple interpretive trajectories, as long as they are expressions of a discipline-from-within. Inspired by Maxine Greene's sense of personal-public freedom, we acknowledge the plurality of voices associated with authentic quests. In the spirit of democratic living—that is, power of, by, for the people, as evoked by Dewey (1938/1998): "to paraphrase the saying of Lincoln about democracy, one of education of, by, and for experience" (p. 19), we summarily reject all attempts to homogenize and standardize human understanding and expression, and we recognize that such attempts are grounded in an authoritarian logic.

Now that we have clarified our approach to "professional discipline," we want to present three disciplinary dimensions that follow naturally from our C&P mission statement. Briefly, they are **deliberative artistry, diversified inquiry**, and **democratic fidelity** as informed by the scholarship of Joseph Schwab, John Dewey, Alain Badiou and, of course, many others.

Schwab's (1969, 1971, 1973, & 1983) four essays on how the "arts of the practical" are informed by the "arts of the eclectic" and how these arts are practiced in educational settings serves as a historic referent for **deliberative artistry** in curriculum work. Such curriculum artistry requires a particular discipline-from-within that has been ably examined, explored and applied by a number of curriculum scholars including Decker Walker, Gail McCutcheon and William Reid. For example, McCutcheon (1995) writes:

> In short, deliberation is a complicated yet organized approach to making curriculum decisions, not merely a discussion or debate about curriculum. …In making curriculum decisions it is important to consider four bodies of knowledge accompanied by specialized knowledge of curriculum development. These four bodies of knowledge are about the "commonplaces" called students, subject matter, the milieu, and teachers. The curriculum specialist facilitates the process of curriculum development by calling attention to these commonplaces and by guiding the group to examine in detail their decisions and curriculum bits such as a curriculum guide, syllabus, graded course of study, or curriculum materials. (p. 28)

Extending Gail McCutcheon's comprehensive approach to curriculum decision-making, Henderson and Gornik (2007) argue that educators' deliberative artistry should, as much as possible, be "systemic" by addressing the interrelationships between designing, planning, teaching, evaluating and organizing decisions.

A particular "arc" in John Dewey's philosophical scholarship serves as a historic referent for **diversified inquiry**. This arc begins with Dewey's

(1897/2004) articulation of his pedagogical beliefs/actions, reviewed in contemporary terms by Tanner (1997), then moves to his diversified study of "educative experience," and concludes with his deliberations on "culture" as, perhaps, a better focus for his inquiries into educative experience (Jackson, 2002). [6] This key arc in Dewey's highly productive scholarly career provides a vivid illustration of disciplined inquiry guided by an open set of inquiry modes [epistemological, ethical, poetic, political, ...] focusing on the democratization of human experience, or what Green (1999) calls "deep democracy." In effect, Dewey models a discipline-from-within that is positioned at the intersection of pedagogical beliefs/actions, emancipatory experiences, and the promise of democratic culture. He is practicing a highly diversified inquiry that is informed by a "love of wisdom" and that is directed toward the democratization of educational experience (Garrison, 1997; Henderson & Kesson, 2004).

Finally, Alain Badiou's sophisticated philosophical project serves as a recent historic referent for **democratic fidelity**. Badiou (2001) provides precise definitions for his key ontological concepts of "situation" and "event." He writes that all human situations are complex, open-ended phenomena that recede into infinity. Hence, no one can claim that they have acquired an over-view of a particular situation. However, individuals can experience an event in a particular situation that inspires them to speak a truth "for all." Such a truth can be interpreted as "democratic" in the sense that it includes all humanity and, even, all species on the planet (Badiou, 2005a). This truth inspiration, which endures after the specific event has occurred, "compels the subject to invent a new way of being and acting in the situation" (pp. 41-42). Badiou (2001) elaborates:

> Essentially, a truth is the material course traced, within the situation, by the eventual supplementation. It is thus an *immanent break*. 'Immanent' because a truth proceeds *in* the situation, and nowhere else—there is no heaven of truths. ...I call 'subject' the bearer...of a fidelity, the one who bears a process of truth. The subject, therefore, in no way pre-exists the process. He [or she] is absolutely nonexistent in the situation 'before' the event. We might say that the process of truth *induces* a subject. (pp. 42-43, author's emphasis)

---

[6] We wish to remind our readers that Dewey makes no distinction between believing, acting and experiencing. See, for example, Dewey's (1904) examination of the relationship between theory and practice in education. In effect, this 1904 essay anticipates Schwab's notion of the "practical" in curriculum work sixty-five years before the publication of Schwab's first essay on his concept.

Badiou's point is that such subjectivities are constructed in the context of particular "for all" inspirations and that the truth processes that emerge out of these personal inspirations are both inclusive/universal and contingent/partial.

Badiou's concept of ethical fidelity advances two key hallmarks of democratic living. First, there is a humility embedded in his ethics that is quite consistent with a Socratic love of wisdom. Badiou (1988/2005b) situates his ethics at the edge of the "void"—at the edge of an 'I don't know' that recedes into infinity. For Badiou, every "situation" is constituted by an infinite set of elements, and humans must learn to be comfortable with complexity and mystery. From an onto-logical point of view, they have no choice. Certainly, humans must construct/make meaning to live purposeful lives, but it is important that they recognize that, often, what they consider to be 'solid' is actually an "appearance" (Badiou, 2006) that is, always already, leaking into infinity (Badiou, 2005c). Such is human fate. We cannot be wise; we can only engage in a disciplined love of wisdom.

Second, Badiou's focuses on an existential "subjectification" that is powerfully modeled by Maxine Greene. No one gets to play 'god'; and in the context of a pluralistic "ethics of truth," anyone can speak "for all" as long as they persevere in their perspective without succumbing to technical superficialities, denials of complexity, ideological impositions, and other related abnegations of the subjective-universal dynamic. We think that the result of such disciplined "subjectification," if it was ever to occur beyond Socrates, Confucius, Buddha, Laozi, Jesus, Rabbi Hillel, and other historically significant, inspirational teachers (Armstrong, 2006), would be the realization of a cultural renaissance embodied in what Dewey (1929/1999) characterizes as "new individualism." Badiou's philosophical project provides insight into a vital, contemplative discipline-from-within. Without educators who can sustain inclusive, "for all" ethical commitments, there doesn't seem to be much hope for the future of democracy in education. In sum, the C&P mission challenges all of us to enact/embody democratic fidelity, and Badiou's ethics informs this disciplinary challenge.

Advancing these three dimensions of C&P "disciplinarity" (Pinar, 2007) can be a useful leadership strategy. After listening to a presentation of the C&P mission and its underlying discipline, the Curriculum and Instruction (C&I) faculty at Kent State University has decided to organize the NCATE-mandated assessment of the C&I Master's Degree Program in accordance with the following design:

Though all of the College and Graduate School of Education's C&I Master's Degree courses are designed to facilitate "critical reflection experiences" (CRE), the C&I faculty has identified three key "transition points" for purposes of CRE assessment. These are: C&I 6/77001 entitled "Fundamentals of Curriculum," a capstone course/experience entitled "Critical Reflections in C&I," and a post-graduate questionnaire to be administered three years after the completion of "Critical Reflections in C&I." C&I Master's Degree students take C&I 6/77001 at the earliest possible point in their program and the capstone course/experience at the latest possible point in their program. The capstone experience can also be completed as a summer semester independent study or as part of a thesis project. The CRE assessments are based on the following standard:

Educators will demonstrate the necessary knowledge and skills to inspire, facilitate and sustain a democratic, curriculum-based pedagogy.

This standard is achieved through the cultivation of three forms of discipline-from-within, conceptualized along vertical, horizontal and diagonal planes:

- The vertical plane: engaging in a diversified study of historical and current topics that inform curriculum-based pedagogy.

- The horizontal plane: practicing the arts of deliberative judgment associated with curriculum-based pedagogy.

- The diagonal plane — undertaking the arts of contemplating and embodying democratic fidelity in curriculum-based pedagogy.

Our evaluation of this standard is based on the following premises:

- Our evaluation approach fosters a disciplined openness consistent with professional responsibility. We recognize that external accountability systems are grounded in an authoritarian logic and encourage semi-professional dispositions. Furthermore, we recognize that evaluation premised on disciplined openness contains an underlying democratic logic consistent with our standard.

- The three forms of internal discipline are conceptualized as situated on planes of immanence that generate multiple lines of flight. In effect, we encourage non-linear, recursive interpretive trajectories that are "kaleidoscopic" in scope and expression.

- These disciplined study/practice/self-exploration interactions are informed by productive idiosyncrasy with its celebration of diverse expressive outcomes.

- The assessment of such dynamic "moving targets" requires the use of an open-ended set of personally and contextually relevant indicators. We have created general indicators of personalized movement within and between the three planes. Such indicators are necessary referents for graduate students without a strong sense of C&I disciplinarity. However, we encourage those graduate students, who embrace C&I disciplinarity, to generate their own personalized indicators.

- The assessment allows for a broad range of interpretations on what constitutes "subject matter content."

The C&I faculty at Kent State University are currently finalizing the details of enacting this as-sessment design. Though these details may be of some interest to journal readers, they are not the point of our story. We want all the readers of this journal to understand that the C&P mission possesses an underlying discipline-from-within that can inform our curriculum leadership advances and that there are specific illustrations of this "discipline" in this issue as well as in all of the other issues of our journal.

References

Armstrong, K. (2006). *The great transformation: The beginning of our religious traditions*. New York: Alfred A. Knopf.
Badiou, A. (2001). *Ethics: An essay on the understanding of evil* (P. Hallward, Trans.). London: Verso.
Badiou, A. (2005a). *Metapolitics* (J. Barker, Trans.). London: Verso.
Badiou, A. (2005b). *Being and event* (O. Feltham, Trans.). New York: Continuum. (Original work published 1988)
Badiou, A. (2005c). *Infinite thought: Truth and the return to philosophy* (O. Feltham & J. Clemens, Trans. & Eds.). London: Continuum.
Badiou, A. (2006). *Theoretical writings* (R. Brassier and A. Toscano, Trans. & Eds.). London: Continuum.
Cherryholmes, C. H. (1988). *Power and criticism: Poststructural investigations in education*. New York: Teachers College Press.
Deleuze, G., & Guattari, F. (1987). *A thousand plateaus: Capitalism and schizophrenia* (B. Massumi, Trans.). Minneapolis: University of Minnesota Press. (Original work published 1980)
Dewey, J. (1904). The relation of theory to practice in education. In C. A. McMurry (Ed.), *The relation of theory to practice in the education of teachers* (Third Yearbook of the National Society for the Scientific Study of Education, Part 1, pp. 9-30). Chicago: University of Chicago Press.

Dewey, J. (1998). *Experience and education.* West Lafayette, IN: Kappa Delta Pi. (Original work published 1938)

Dewey, J. (1999). *Individualism old and new.* Amherst, NY: Prometheus Books. (Original work published 1929)

Dewey, J. (2004). My pedagogic creed. In D. J. Flinders & S. J. Thornton (Eds.), *The curriculum studies reader* (2nd ed., pp. 17-23). New York: Routledge-Falmer. (Original work published 1897)

Eisner, E. W. (1994). The educational imagination: On the design and evaluation of school programs (3rd ed.). New York: Macmillan. (Original work published 1979)

Ford, G. W., & Pugno, L. (Eds.). (1964). *The structure of knowledge and the curriculum.* Chicago: Rand McNally and Company.

Foucault, M. (1980). Truth and power. In C. Gordon (Ed.), *Power/knowledge: Selected interviews and other writings 1972-1977* (pp. 109-133). New York: Pantheon Books.

Garrison, J. (1997). *Dewey and eros: Wisdom and desire in the art of teaching.* New York: Teachers College Press.

Green, J. M. (1999). *Deep democracy: Community, diversity, and transformation.* Lanham, MD: Rowman & Littlefield.

Greene, M. (1988). *The dialectic of freedom.* New York: Teachers College Press.

Henderson, J. G., & Gornik, R. (2007). *Transformative curriculum leadership* (3rd ed.). Upper Saddle River, NJ: Merrill/Prentice Hall.

Henderson, J. G., & Kesson, K. R. (2004). *Curriculum wisdom: Educational decisions in democratic societies.* Upper Saddle River, NJ: Merrill/Prentice Hall.

Jackson, P. W. (2002). *John Dewey and the philosopher's task.* New York: Teachers College Press.

Kreisberg, S. (1992). *Transforming power: Domination, empowerment, and education.* Albany, NY: SUNY Press.

McCutcheon, G. (1995). *Developing the curriculum: Solo and group deliberation.* White Plains, NY: Longman.

Pinar, W. F. (2007). *Intellectual advancement through disciplinarity: Verticality and horizontality in curriculum studies.* Rotterdam: Sense Publishers.

Schwab, J. J. (1969). The practical: A language for curriculum. *School Review 78*(1), 1-23.

Schwab, J. J. (1971). The practical: Arts of the eclectic. *School Review, 79*, 493-542.

Schwab, J. J. (1973). The practical 3: Translation into curriculum. *School Review, 81*, 501-522.

Schwab, J. J. (1983). The practical 4: Something for curriculum professors to do. *Curriculum Inquiry, 13*, 239-266.

Tanner, L. N. (1997). *Dewey's laboratory school: Lessons for today.* New York: Teachers College Press.

Uhrmacher, P. B., & Matthews, J. (2005). Building his palette of scholarship: A biographical sketch of Elliot Eisner. In P. B. Uhrmacher & J. Matthews

(Eds.), *Intricate palette: Working the ideas of Elliot Eisner* (pp. 1-13). Upper Saddle River, NJ: Merrill/Prentice Hall.

van Manen, M. (1991). *The tact of teaching: The meaning of pedagogical thoughtfulness.* Albany, NY: SUNY Press.

Evaluating a Pragmatic Understanding of Artistry, Development, and Leadership

This Editors' Introduction (Volume 5, Number 2) began with a set of self-evaluative questions. These questions emerge out of an ongoing series of pragmatic explanations and clarifications of the Curriculum and Pedagogy Group's mission statement, which we initiated in the first issue of *JCP*[7], and to start this essay we will provide a brief "map" of the territory we have covered. Our goal has been to examine the implications of democratic education for pedagogical artistry, professional development, and curriculum leadership; and we have pursued this goal by drawing on the North American pragmatic heritage, particularly as informed by John Dewey's scholarship.

With reference to pedagogical artistry, we have explored the linkage between democratic vocational callings and educational artistry as articulated by Dewey (1897/2004):

> Education ... is a process of living and not a preparation for future living. ... Much of present education fails because it neglects this fundamental principle of the school as a form of [democratic] community life. ... Education thus conceived marks the most perfect and intimate union of science and art conceivable in human experience. The art of thus giving shape to human powers and adapting them to social service is the supreme art; one calling into its service the best of artists; that no insight, sympathy, tact, executive power, is too great for such a service. Every teacher should realize the dignity of his [or her] calling. (pp. 18–19, 23)

---

[7] For this journal's explication of the Curriculum and Pedagogy Group's mission statement, see Appendix A.

We recognize that education can be treated as an applied social science, as illustrated by the "No Child Left Behind" Act and by a host of other dominant and domineering twentieth-and twenty-first-century policy instruments. However, we think this mainstream view of education is not only limiting but demeaning, and we resonate with Dewey's vision of educational service. We celebrate those educators who feel "called" to democratic education and who, therefore, embrace educational work as a form of inspired human artistry. We recognize that these educators-as-artists are necessarily committed to the expressive subtleties and mysteries of their own unique, authentic professional calling. Eisner's (1994) notion of "productive idiosyncrasy" is the frame of reference for their work and their students' learning; and whenever possible, they establish critical distance from the incessant pressures to conform and standardize. Many of the contributions in the current Curriculum and Pedagogy Conference Proceedings (Fidyk, Wallin, & den Heyer, 2008) provide vivid illustrations of the linkage between personal democratic callings and pedagogical artistry.

With reference to professional development, we have conceptualized three forms of disciplined artistry. First, there are the arts of deliberation that underlie sophisticated problem solving. Democratic education is necessarily respectful of each individual student's talents and abilities, requiring educators to proceed on a caring, case-by-case basis (Noddings, 1984). Attempts to straightjacket and label students in accordance with one-size-fits-all solutions, ideological agendas, and/or sorting mechanisms must be critically challenged. To the degree possible, democratic educators need to enact a practical, eclectic artistry in a spirit of open-minded collaboration and negotiation (Schwab, 1978). Second, there are the arts of inquiry that underlie the study of the complex, multidimensional relationships between educational experience and "deep democracy" (Green, 1999). This work requires "complicated conversation," as advanced by Pinar, Reynolds, Slattery, and Taubman (1995) and Slattery (2006) in their synoptic texts, and diversified questioning, as advanced by Henderson and Kesson (2004) in their inquiry map. Finally, there are the arts of fidelity required to embody democracy-in-education. As a place marker for enduring ideals the term "democracy" is abstract, remote, and vague; however, when embodied in the here and now of specific educational events, it comes alive. Badiou's (2001) discussion of ethics as inspirational awakening, existential commitment, and "for all" action pro-vides valuable insight into this form of disciplined artistry.[8] De-

---

[8] For an extended discussion of Badiou's ethics as inspired by Dewey's scholarship, see Kesson and Henderson (2010).

mocratic educators will need to work hard to develop their deliberative, inquiry, and fidelity artistries. It will require years—perhaps a lifetime—of dedicated, continuing studies; and in our last editors' introduction, we provided an illustration of how this disciplined professional development is initiated and encouraged in Kent State University's Curriculum and Instruction Master's Degree Program.[9]

With reference to curriculum leadership, we have discussed a set of interrelated educational practices as presented in Henderson and Gornik (2007), and all six activities are specific applications of the three forms of disciplined artistry that we have just reviewed:

- **reconceptualizing** educational standards—rethinking teaching responsibilities from a democracy-in-education perspective;

- **engaging** in reflective inquiry—integrating reflective practice with diversified inquiry into the relationship between democracy and education;

- **undertaking** personal examination—cultivating democratic ethical fidelity;

- **building** learning communities—sustaining disciplined professional development and stakeholder learning;

- **enacting** systemic deliberation—integrating designing, planning, teaching, evaluating, and organizing decisions; and

- **commencing** public intellectual leadership—attempting to inspire the public imagination about the meaning of quality education in a "deepening" democracy.

The more educators develop their deliberative, inquiry, and fidelity capacities, the better they will be able to engage in these six interrelated activities; and therefore, the better they can function as inspired educational artists in this particular way.

With this review of our pragmatic understanding of pedagogical artistry, professional development, and curriculum leadership, we now pose a set of self-evaluative questions. We recognize that these questions are not a defini-

---

[9] Laurel Chehayl (2008) has provided leadership for the design and implementation of a similar Master's Degree Program at Monmouth University. Additional undergraduate and graduate program applications are currently under discussion at two state universities and one private college.

tive list. Additional inquiries could be entertained and pursued in light of our conception of democratic curriculum-based pedagogy or with reference to an alternative conception. Acknowledging these limitations, we offer these questions as an invitation to practice the arts of self-evaluation. With reference to disciplined deliberation, these arts draw practically and eclectically on a wide range of discourse-practices concerning such related matters as personal reflection, self-examination, autobiographical analysis, contemplation, meditation, and narrative expression. Pinar's (2004) argument for curriculum as "currere" and Nash's (2004) presentation of a method for practicing "scholarly personal narratives" serve as two illustrations of such discourse-practices. For the purpose of conceptual convenience, the questions are divided into pedagogical artistry, professional development, and curriculum leadership sections. However, in the dynamic flow of lived experience such divisions are artificial. The questions naturally bleed into one another.

Pedagogical Artistry

Do I experience a call to enact democracy in education? If so, how do I experience this calling? What are my inspirations? With reference to Dewey's *My Pedagogical Creed*, how do I understand the "dignity" of this calling, and how do I understand the linkage between my vocational calling and pedagogical artistry? How might I explain this linkage to my colleagues, particularly those who view education as an applied science containing a broad set of "best practice" crafts? How do I establish critical distance from educational policies that are predicated on the standardized management of teachers? Where do I find the leverage and the "wiggle room" to work in a spirit of productive idiosyncrasy? What am I doing to cultivate my sense of pedagogical artistry?

Professional Development

How do I understand education as a discipline, and am I developing my disciplinary capacities in accordance with my understanding? Am I part of a formal or informal disciplined professional learning community? Do I have "critical friends" who encourage and support my disciplined professional development? Is "professional development" even a useful term to describe my continuing growth efforts? If not, what is a better term? Do I resonate with the three descriptions of educators' disciplined artistry? If so, how am I continuously refining my deliberative, inquiry, and fidelity artistries? If I attend the annual Curriculum and Pedagogy Conference, do I experience this professional meeting as an opportunity to work on my disciplined artistries? How do I evaluate the "quality" of my professional development, and how would I justify this qualitative awareness to my colleagues and other curriculum and pedagogy stakeholders?

Curriculum Leadership

In light of my sense of professional artistry and discipline, do I distinguish between instructional leadership with its limited focus on "best" practices and a more comprehensive curriculum leadership? If so, how do I practice curriculum leadership? With reference to the "reconceptualist" heritage in curriculum studies with its focus on the complexities and subtleties of educational experience, have I reconceptualized my "subject matter" instructional responsibilities? If so, how have I done this? Can I undertake the necessary complicated conversations and diversified inquiries and then integrate this multitextual and multidimensional curricular awareness into my reflective problem solving? In more succinct terms, can I practice the requisite reflective inquiry? If so, how would I explain the distinction between instructional reflection and curriculum-based reflective inquiry to my colleagues and other interested stakeholders? How do I maintain a sense of "democratic" integrity in all aspects of my curriculum and pedagogy work? How am I voicing my own inspired awareness of democratic education, and how am I listening to the inspired voices of other democratic educators? How do I sustain my hopes and visions in these trying times? What keeps me going? Do I work on building formal or informal disciplined learning communities? Is so, how? If not, how do I work on cultivating my professional artistries? How do I understand educational ecology; and based on this understanding, how do I practice systemic deliberation and encourage my colleagues to be sensitive to the interdependence of the fundamentals of curriculum work? How do I encourage collaboration and negotiation? In short, how do I promote the necessary ecological awareness and dialogical openness? In what public arenas, large or small, do I exercise leadership? How am I attempting to influence and inspire the public imagination on what constitutes "quality" education?

References

Badiou, A. (2001). *Ethics: An essay on the understanding of evil* (P. Hallward, Trans.). London: Verso.

Chehayl, L. (2008, October). *Because they must dance: Supporting teachers' democratic curriculum leadership in an institutional environment.* Paper presented at the Annual Bergamo Conference on Curriculum Theory and Classroom Practice, Dayton, OH.

Dewey, J. (2004). My pedagogic creed. In D. J. Flinders & S. J. Thornton (Eds.), *The curriculum studies reader* (2nd ed., pp. 17-23). New York: Routledge-Falmer. (Original work published 1897)

Eisner, E. W. (1994). *The educational imagination: On the design and evaluation of school programs* (3rd ed.). New York: Macmillan.

Fidyk, A., Wallin, J., & den Heyer, K. (Eds.). (2008). *Democratizing educational experience: Envisioning, embodying, enacting.* Troy, NY: Educator's International Press.

Green, J. M. (1999). *Deep democracy: Community, diversity, and transformation.* Lanham, MD: Rowman & Littlefield.

Henderson, J. G., & Gornik, R. (2007). *Transformative curriculum leadership* (3rd ed.). Upper Saddle River, NJ: Merrill/Prentice Hall.

Henderson, J. G., & Kesson, K. R. (2004). *Curriculum wisdom: Educational decisions in democratic societies.* Upper Saddle River, NJ: Merrill/Prentice Hall.

Kesson, K. R., & Henderson, J. G. (2010). Reconceptualizing professional development for curriculum leadership: Inspired by John Dewey and informed by Alain Badiou. *Educational Philosophy and Theory, 42*(2), 213-229.

Nash, R. J. (2004). *Liberating scholarly writing: The power of personal narrative.* New York: Teachers College Press.

Noddings, N. (1984). *Caring: A feminine approach to ethics and moral education.* Berkeley: University of California Press.

Pinar, W. F. (2004). *What is curriculum theory?* Mahwah, NJ: Lawrence Erlbaum Associates.

Pinar, W. F., Reynolds, W. M., Slattery, P., & Taubman, P. M. (1995). *Understanding curriculum: An introduction to the study of historical and contemporary curriculum discourses.* New York: Peter Lang.

Schwab, J. J. (1978). *Science, curriculum, and liberal education: Selected essays* (I. Westbury & N. J. Wilkof, Eds.). Chicago: University of Chicago Press.

Slattery, P. (2006). *Curriculum development in the postmodern era* (2nd ed.). New York: Routledge.

Exploring an Evolving Field

Over the past six years, the Editors' Introductions have presented extended commentary on the notion of democratic, curriculum-based pedagogy. We think this concept captures the essence of our journal's mission statement as well as the Curriculum & Pedagogy Group's professional vision. Our referent for "democratic" education has been the heritage of North American pragmatism, particularly as articulated by John Dewey. For example, we agree with Dewey's (1939/1989) position that "democracy is a way of personal life which provides a moral standard for personal conduct" (p. 101). We are not surprised that Dewey felt that "culture" might be a better organizing term for his scholarship than "experience" because we also subscribe to this comprehensive approach to democracy-in-education. We think that, to the degree possible, curriculum settings should be designed to serve as special cultural sites of democratic living, and we agree with Dewey that the curricular focus should be on providing students with democratic experiences in the here-and-now of their educational lives and not in some vague, promised future. After reviewing a wide range of historical and current definitions of human artistry, Dissanayake (1988) argues that the essence of art is "making special" (p. 92). She elaborates: "One intends by making special to place the activity or artifact in a 'realm' different from the everyday" (p. 92). Though students' everyday lives may not be particularly "democratic" in any sense of the word, democratic educators are not deterred. They are committed to providing their students with the special curricular experiences they need to begin to understand the personal and social responsibilities of democratic living.

Our referent for "curriculum" has been the reconceptualist heritage in curriculum studies (Pinar, 1975), which has evolved into a wide range of post-reconceptualist projects (Malewski, 2010). We agree with Pinar, Reynolds, Slattery, and Taubman (1995) that "curriculum is an extraordinarily complicated conversation" (p. 848), and we emphatically reject the simplistic, standardized engineering "logic" that dominates curriculum work in today's educational institutions. We resonate with Cherryholmes's (1988) and Kliebard's (1992) astute critiques of the Tyler Rationale (Tyler, 1949), and we invite educators to cultivate the creative "imagination" (Eisner, 1994; Fesmire, 2003), the "eclectic" arts (Schwab, 1978), and the "postmodern" hermeneutic sensibilities (Slattery, 2006) that are required to interpret visions of democracy-in-education for curriculum enactment. In sum, we encourage complicated conversations on the meaning of "democratic education" and complicated deliberations and continuous self-examinations on how these meanings can be embodied in aesthetically powerful and transparently faithful ways.

Finally, our referent for "pedagogy" has been Dewey's (1934/1958) art as experience, which involves "the capacity of experience to be transformed so as to be wholly integrated, to be an experience. Such experience includes emotion, expression, form, quality, and communication" (Alexander, 1987, p. 276). Alexander (1987) notes that Dewey felt that such passionate and well-integrated transactions served as his paradigm for educational experience:

> [An experience] marks the moment when nature becomes culture, that is, nature's potentiality for embodying meaning and value have been consummatorily fulfilled through action. Such moments have high moral significance for Dewey because they indicate that nature contains these possibilities, if not as self-complete, autonomous entities, then at the very least as ideals which may be striven for by the arts of intelligence. (p. 267)

We invite a critical reading of all Curriculum & Pedagogy (C&P) artifacts from the perspective of democratic curriculum-based pedagogy. An extended version of our analysis of the notions of curriculum and pedagogy can be found in the introduction to the ninth proceedings of the Curriculum and Pedagogy Conference. However, for this short journal introduction we will continue with our perspective on the curriculum studies field.

Within this Editors' Introduction we wanted to offer our view of the curriculum studies field. First, and most important, we do not see the curriculum field and its history as cohesive. Categories and histories of curriculum studies are complex, contested, and fluid. Consider curriculum conferences and journals, for example. We have been active in the curriculum field since the early 1980s. We have regularly presented papers and attended sessions at AERA Divisions A, B, K, and G. We have served as leaders and speakers in various SIG's at AERA, including Arts-Based Educational Research, Qualitative Studies in Education, Religion and Education, Critical Issues in Curriculum and Instruction, Chaos and Complexity, Spirituality and Education, Queer Studies, and many others. While Division B might be considered our "academic home" at AERA, we have not limited our research and papers to Division B. We have attended and presented papers at C&P, AATC, AAACS, ABER, LSU Curriculum Camp, ASCD, the Bergamo Conference, Professors of Curriculum, AESA, and many other curriculum conferences for over twenty-five years in addition to AERA Divisions A, B, K, and G and related SIGS. We have also published our work in a wide range of curriculum journals, AERA publications, generalist educational magazines, and related interdisciplinary scholarly journals. As we have attended conferences and published papers, we have encountered colleagues from across the philosophical spectrum in every venue. And what is most interesting is that colleagues and graduate students move in and out of conference participation, AERA divisions and SIGS, and publishing venues on a regular basis.

There does not appear, to us, to be a cohesive or identifiable reason why academics and graduate students attend C&P, Bergamo, AAACS, AATC, the Purdue Conference, IAACS, AESA, ASCD, or AERA. Colleagues appear on the program at AERA in various divisions and SIGS across the spectrum from year to year. We do not detect absolute ideological or theoretical consistency in the conferences and journals in the curriculum field. Attendance at a conference appears to be, from our perspective, based more on location, conference theme, funding, timing, friendships, recommendations from colleagues, invitations to speak, and other personal intangibles. Our point is this: we do not detect philosophical cohesion in the curriculum conferences and curriculum journals. We have published papers with the same methodology and philosophy in both the *Journal of Curriculum Studies* and *JCT*; *Educational Researcher and Curriculum Inquiry*; *Harvard Educational Review*, and *JCP*. Our philosophical and theoretical orientations are similar whether we present papers at C&P, AATC, AAACS, IAACS, UCEA, Bergamo, Professors of Curriculum, ABER, or AESA.

The curriculum field is contested, and curriculum conferences have been divisive at times. Political scholars, queer scholars, feminist scholars, and others have found one conference or another more welcoming to their perspectives and personalities — perhaps because of a collaborative project or travel and budget constraints. We do not find, for example, the "Curriculum and Pedagogy Conference" or "Professors of Curriculum" or the "American Association for the Advancement of Curriculum Studies" or the "Bergamo Conference on Curriculum Theory and Classroom Practice" or the "LSU Curriculum Camp" or "The Purdue Conference on Post-Reconceptualization" to be sufficiently different in their theoretical and philosophical orientations to constitute a unique or cohesive curricular entity. Attendance is open to the field; anyone can submit papers. In fact, in any given year we will encounter colleagues who attend, perhaps, four conferences — Professors of Curriculum, AAACS, Bergamo, and AERA Division B one year; C&P, AESA, Professors of Curriculum, and ASCD the next year; C&P, IAACS, AERA Division G, and AATC the next year, and so on. Our own personal experience is that we attend 3 or 4 conferences a year and publish two or three journal manuscripts a year, and every year we have a different collection of conferences and journals. We shift; we move. We are not static. And we see a different set of colleagues and graduate students from across the philosophical spectrum at every conference. In sum, we do not experience any mission or membership cohesion in the curriculum field. Certainly there are "regulars" at every conference, but even "regulars" drop out of sight from time to time, and new graduate students become "regulars." The field is fluid, evolving, and shifting at every moment. Also, the reasons for participation in the various components of the field have less to do with mission statements and ideology, and more to do with personalities, habits, logistics, friendships, funding, publishing opportunities, invitations to collaborate, and the like.

So what does all of this mean? Is the mission statement of C&P that we discussed above and in previous Editors' Introductions to *JCP* irrelevant? No. Our mission statement for C&P and *JCP* was formulated with transparent and democratic intents—and we were successful at times and we fell short at other times. Our mission statements are living documents, open to revision and interpretation. Not all participants agree with the mission statement. Not all scholars who publish in this journal or attend C&P agree on all aspects of the stated philosophy. In fact, many people critique and amend the documents over time. We believe that this is healthy. The mission statement is not the final word, nor is it an indication of agreement or cohesion. This is the tenth anniversary year of C&P and the sixth volume of *JCP*. As scholars who were a part of the initial organizers of C&P and *JCP* in 1999, we do not see ourselves or this organization in opposition to any other journal or conference. We see ourselves as two scholars with a commitment to the curriculum studies field in all of its diversity. C&P and *JCP* provide one outlet for papers, publications, career advancement, and community friendship. The same is true for all of the other journals and conferences in the field. Curriculum Studies is a relatively small field, and the multiplicity of various journals and conferences is a healthy dimension of the field.

We find the curriculum field to be an exciting and engaging home for our scholarship and career precisely because it is interdisciplinary, fluid, evolving, complex, and contested. We appreciate diversity of scholarship and the emergence of new and disruptive patterns in all of our conferences and journals. We resist notions of cohesion or unity in the curriculum field and in the conferences and journals. It was therefore a challenge for us, as co-editors, to remain open to nuances and possibilities from all sectors of the field and not limit scholarship or scholars based on preconceived categories. As we end our tenure in 2010 as co-editors of *JCP*, we look forward to unexpected and unplanned projects in the field in the years ahead. We welcome Stephanie Springgay and Steve Carpenter as the new co-editors of *JCP*. They will bring fresh energy and new directions to this journal and to the field. We look forward to their leadership.

References

Alexander, T. M. (1987). *John Dewey's theory of art, experience and nature: The horizons of feeling*. Albany, NY: State University of New York Press.

Cherryholmes, C. H. (1988). *Power and criticism: Poststructural investigations in education*. New York: Teachers College Press.

Dissanayake, E. (1988). *What is art for?* Seattle: University of Washington Press.

Dewey, J. (1989). *Freedom and culture*. Buffalo, NY: Prometheus. (Original work published 1939)

Dewey, J. (1958). *Art as experience*. New York: Capricorn Books. (Original work published 1934)

Eisner, E. W. (1994). *The educational imagination: On the design and evaluation of school programs* (3rd ed.). New York: Macmillan.

Ellsworth, E. (2005). *Places of learning: Media, architecture, pedagogy*. New York: Routledge.

Fesmire, S. (2003). *John Dewey and moral imagination: Pragmatism in ethics*. Bloomington, IN: Indiana University Press.

Kliebard, H. K. (1992). *Forging the American curriculum: Essays in curriculum history and theory*. New York: Routledge.

Malewski, E. (Ed.). (2010). *Curriculum studies handbook: The next moment*. New York: Routledge. 185-199.

Pinar, W. F. (Ed.). (1975). *Curriculum theorizing: The reconceptualists*. Berkeley, CA: McCutchan.

Pinar, W. F. (2004). *What is curriculum theory?* Mahwah, New Jersey: Erlbaum Associates.

Pinar, W. F., Reynolds, W. M., Slattery, P., & Taubman, P. M. (1995). *Understanding curriculum: An introduction to the study of historical and contemporary curriculum discourses*. New York: Peter Lang.

Schwab, J. J. (1978). *Science, curriculum, and liberal education: Selected essays* (I. Westbury & N. J. Wilkof, Eds.). Chicago: University of Chicago Press.

Slattery, P. (2006). *Curriculum development in the postmodern era* (2nd ed.). New York: Routledge.

Tyler, R. W. (1949). *Basic principles of curriculum and instruction*. Chicago: University of Chicago Press.

Concluding Thoughts and Reflections

This our final Editors' Introduction was composed with a deep sense of gratitude for all of our current and past editorial staff members, for the current and past members of our editorial board, for the current and past contributors to this journal, for the current and past members of the governing council of Curriculum & Pedagogy Group, and for our publisher, Bill Clockel, and his Educator's International Press staff. Without the devoted efforts of all of these individuals, the *JCP* could not have achieved its current level of excellence and respectability. The initial work on creating a journal dedicated to advancing the relationship between contemporary curriculum studies and pedagogical artistry began about eight years ago, and we have come a long way with this twelfth issue of our journal. It has been a labor of love; and we are confident that the new co-editors, Stephanie Springgay and Stephen Carpenter, will provide the necessary leadership for the journal's continuing advancement. We believe that *JCP* has created a unique and positive contribution to the curriculum field during a time of tremendous transitions in education, politics, culture, economy, and ecology. We are proud of the contributors to *JCP* who have addressed these important themes in each issue of the journal.

From the very beginning of our journal efforts, we have been quite conscious of our responsibility to properly represent and articulate the vision that sustains the Curriculum & Pedagogy Group as a vital professional association. This is why we have incorporated commentary on the notion of *democratic, curriculum-based pedagogy* into all of our editors' introductions. As we stated a number of times throughout our editors' introductions, we think this concept captures the essence of our journal's mission statement and the Curriculum & Pedagogy Group's professional vision. In effect, we have examined and explored the meaning of *democratic, curriculum-based pedagogy* in what is now a book-length set of eleven essays. We summarize this six-year effort in the Foreword that we composed for the ninth annual proceedings of the Curriculum & Pedagogy Conference. In our Foreword, we challenge ourselves, our curriculum and pedagogy colleagues, and all of our journal readers to "understand that...comprehensive study, creative enactment, systemic deliberation and ethical fidelity...are key disciplinary habits that we must daily cultivate" (Henderson & Slattery, 2009, p. xvii).

It is our hope that this understanding of the discipline of education in societies with democratic ideals will be embraced by a growing number of educators and curriculum stakeholders, and we recognize that this hope cannot be realized without the dedicated efforts of curriculum leaders who embody and inspire this discipline. We strongly feel that this is a clear way forward—a 'right action'—for education in the 21st century; and it needs to involve all educators from every ethnic, racial, gender, sexual, socio-economic, cultural, philosophical, geographic, religious, and ability working together. No educator should be denied access to learning the discipline; and conversely, no educator should be excused from the disciplinary duties of the profession.

Dewey (1939/1989) writes: "We have advanced far enough to say that democracy is a way of life. We have yet to realize that it is a way of personal life and one which provides a moral stand-ard for personal conduct" (p. 101). We think Dewey is touching on a key curriculum and pedagogy challenge today. It is time for all citizens in societies with democratic ideals to understand that democracy requires disciplined right action. We feel educators have a key role in realizing this broad, transformative, moral aim. They must take the lead in advancing the discipline of democratic living, and they must exercise this leadership through appropriate, disciplined problem solving practices. In this way, they will shed the semi-professional shackles of their professional heritage, and they will embrace Dewey's (1897/2009) challenge to approach education as the "supreme art" (p. 40).

References

Dewey, J. (1989). *Freedom and culture*. Buffalo, NY: Prometheus. (Original work published 1939)

Dewey, J. (2009). My pedagogic creed. In D. J. Flinders & S. J. Thornton (Eds.), *The curriculum studies reader* (3rd ed., pp. 34-41). New York: Routledge. (Original work published 1897)

Henderson, J. G., & Slattery, P. (2009). Foreword. In J. Burdick, J. A. Sandlin, & T. Daspit, (Eds.), *Complicated conversations and confirmed commitments: Revitalizing education for democracy* (pp. ix-xix). Troy, NY: Educator's International Press.

Part Two

Situating the Town Hall Simulation

JENNIFER L. SCHNEIDER
Kent State University

Part II of this book showcases the diverse scholarly voices of present and past leaders of the Curriculum & Pedagogy (C&P) Group who were invited to participate in a town hall simulation by commenting on the challenges of embodying and enacting the C&P mission. As mentioned in the introductory chapter, they were provided with the following prompt:

> The C&P mission can be succinctly interpreted as advancing the synergistic relationship between disciplined curriculum studies, critical pedagogy and democratic educational leadership. This requires critically-informed educators to cross curriculum, teaching and leadership boundaries in bureaucratically compartmentalized P-12 settings and academically balkanized higher education settings. How do you understand the challenges of enacting this professional vision with ethical fidelity? Stated in a more vernacular way, how can critically-informed educators 'walk' this synergistic mission talk? How can they embody the holistic, integrated change that they seek?

They were asked to respond to this prompt with an essay, a poem, or some other idiosyncratic expressive outcome (Eisner, 1994) that would not exceed 1,000 words. With reference to this book's organizing concept, the town hall simulation was designed to facilitate a set of brief, concise **immanent critiques** of the C&P Group's mission statement.

Louise Allen's essay, *Seeking the Good of the Larger Community: Using Dewey's Critical Pragmatism in Creating Democratic Spaces and Practices in the Curriculum and Pedagogy Conference Town Hall* sets the stage for this simulated dialogue. Through an analysis of such C&P Group artifacts as conference documents and interviews, she presents an insightful historical account of the annual C&P town hall meetings. The eleven contributions that follow Louise's paper provide a wide range of perspectives on the question of "ethical fidelity" (Badiou, 2001) to the C&P Group's mission. The responses include theoretical explanations, critical reflections, autobiographical explorations, poetic expressions, and narrative analyses.

Editing this section of the book was quite challenging, particularly deciding on the arrangement of the contributors' diverse responses. I felt that the Part I strategy of working with thematic subtitles would not be a useful way to portray a simulated 'dialogue'. Consequently, instead of using subtitles, I decided to do the very thing Jim and I want readers to do in this section of the book: imagine. I imagined myself as the moderator of the simulated 'dialogue'. I read each essay response multiple times; sometimes I read them separately and other times sequentially contemplating the viewpoints and authors' voices all the while envisioning how the ideas might flow into and out of one another. The result of my experience is reflected in the organization of the contributors' pieces. My hope is that the final design of the town hall simulation creates a space to reflect on the vital relationship between immanent critique, ethical fidelity, and the C&P Group's mission statement.

References

Badiou, A. (2001). *Ethics: An essay on the understanding of evil* (P. Hallward, Trans.). London: Verso.

Eisner, E. W. (1994). *The educational imagination: On the design and evaluation of school programs* (3rd ed.). New York: Macmillan.

Imagining the Town Hall Simulation

Greetings Participant-Reader:

I wish to extend my warmest welcome to you! It is truly a pleasure to have you walking along this 'path less taken,' and we are excited to have you join us as a co-creator of the meaning of immanent critique in curriculum and pedagogy.

The vision for Part II of this book was to simulate with written texts a 'dialogue' at a Curriculum and Pedagogy (C&P) town hall meeting, and this letter is an invitation for you to participate in a text-based conversation, to examine immanent critique through the words of others, and to encourage you to explore this concept in relationship to your own personal and professional commitments. During the reading experience, I strongly encourage you to activate your imagination. Picture yourself at a town hall meeting, sitting around a table, and sipping a drink while listening to and exchanging ideas with the past and present C&P leaders who lent their viewpoints to this book.

I am hopeful that your experience reading these eleven perspectives will be thought provoking, rewarding, and much more. Again, welcome and enjoy your journey among the various compositions and scholarly voices to come!

Yours Sincerely,

Jennifer L. Schneider

Seeking the Good of the Larger Community: Using Dewey's Critical Pragmatism in Creating Democratic Spaces and Practices in the Curriculum and Pedagogy Conference Town Hall

LOUISE ANDERSON ALLEN
South Carolina State University

Founded in 2000, the Curriculum and Pedagogy (C&P) Group was established by a group of curriculum workers who self identified as representing the second wave of curriculum theorizing. Inviting other scholars to "a different kind of conference," their goal was to reconnect school with theoretical insights and it was intended to focus on "the transformative potential of teacher education, curriculum, and life in schools" (Marshall, Sears, Allen, Roberts, & Schubert, 2007, p. 241). Committed to three guiding principles: democratic governance, transparency, and diversity, C&P has over the past ten years offered a space for those who share a common faith in democracy and a commitment to public moral leadership. Each annual meeting ideally is a space where attendees can deliberate over the "democratization" of experience in education and where they can experience a deliberate engagement with specifically targeted audiences (teachers, administrators, parents, community leaders, policy makers, etc.) about curriculum matters (Allen, 2009, p. 1).

At the heart of this space is the town hall where those who share this common faith become participatory citizens. The guiding principles (noted above) and the town hall differentiate C&P from other small gatherings in such a way that the group works inside and outside of disciplinary boundaries by creating a democratic space - green spaces - in the town hall where conference participants may engage in complicated conversations (Pinar, Reynolds, Slattery, & Taubman, 1995, p. 848) about curricular democratic practices. In essence, the town hall is the embodiment of the conscience of the organization.

This paper will seek to explore and document the evolution of the C&P town hall from 2000-2009 through an analysis of the Council records (Allen, 2009), through the conference publications, interviews with founders, and other archival materials. As the conference has grown in size, and moved between retreat-like settings and urban conference centers, and as the membership of the governing Council has changed over the past ten years, the conference has evolved but the one constant has been the town hall and the use of panels to engage the conference attendees in a public dialogue inspired by the common moral purpose of Dewey's moral way of living (1929/1989).

The purpose of the town hall is not to showcase one scholar as a star in the field but to allow panels of scholars to explore the democratic theory and practice of curriculum studies along with the audience (Allen, 2009). By creating a community of discourse in the town hall, the audience is engaged through small groups, reader responders and other methods of audience inclusion. Thus, the town hall is a public space where the audience works in a collaborative nature with the panel in exploring the "complicated conversation" about curriculum (Pinar et al., 1995), while seeking the good of the larger community of not just C&P but also of the curriculum field itself.

Theoretical Framework

This concept of the good of the larger community was of paramount importance to Dewey's educational philosophy (Allen, 2006). In fact, Zilversmit (1993) asserts that "community permeated Dewey's educational thought" (p. 6). The lessons in the classroom were intended to teach the concept of community whereby the students viewed the school as an "embryonic community where children could learn skills experientially as well as from books....which would enable them to work cooperatively in a democratic society" (Semel, 1999, p. 6). Dewey believed that schools should reflect the community, thus the American ideal of democracy should be taught, modeled, and lived.

In much the same way, the founders of C&P have used this concept of the embryonic community to inform and create a conference based on a common faith in democracy, citing Dewey, Maxine Greene, George Counts, Alice Miel, and Horace Mann Bond as the foundational curriculum scholars who frame the public moral dimension of the work of C&P. In its first program, the C&P Group called for curriculum studies to become part of the fabric of public life and connected to "everyday curricular and pedagogical practices" (Preamble, 2000 C&P Conference Program).

This concept is also mirrored in how C&P constructed the Town Hall as reflective of the community of the C&P membership to include graduate students, faculty and practitioners. From the first town halls in 2000, conference meetings have attempted to reconnect curriculum studies to that everyday curricular life (Allen, 2009). The first town hall in 2000 focused on how the shifting coalitions of curriculum workers had crafted spaces to explore, critique, and create different kinds of communities of discourse that could impact the field. Based upon the following five generational lessons, one can easily argue that they represent an example of Dewey's critical pragmatism whereby the founders of C&P deliberately engaged in a "search for knowledge [as a quest] for solutions to practical problems" (Rohmann, 1999, p. 312).

- Consciously and actively network and mentor curriculum workers who attend;

- Invite, promote, and value dissimilar positions and perspectives among participants;

- Explicitly concern ourselves in recognizable and important ways with the multiple contexts that "surround" curriculum work (e.g., political, legal, cultural, economic, social);

- Invite, promote, and value participants representing the broad range of curriculum work (from theorizing and policy deliberation, to planning and enactment; and

- Provide personal and professional benefits to particular individuals and groups within the field.

For these scholars, the act of choosing a means, i.e., the town hall was both a moral and effective way to get to certain, effective ends—creating a different kind of conference without star speakers.

As noted in the C&P mission statement, Dewey undergirds much of the thoughtful reflective planning that created the conference structure. His recognition that human action, particularly new action that disrupts habits and customs—such as the typical conference, comes out of a deep desire for change (1932). And for the founders of C&P, that meant promoting and valuing dissimilar positions and perspectives as noted above with the hope of disrupting the status quo in the curriculum field and reconsidering it toward more critical ends.

In planning the second conference, the Council Chair and the Chair of the Town Hall Committee reported to Council that "We will return with open Town Meetings next year [2001] that are connected directly to the conference theme and hosted by a combination of graduate students and faculty/practitioners" (Allen, 2009, p. 2). Again in 2002, the liaison committee pointed out to Council "we need to be communicating with organizers of town hall meetings and the program chair about planning specific times and events that will engage practicing teachers and administrators, and that will give them times and places to find one another" (Allen, 2009, p. 4). For the fifth anniversary in 2004, the program chair reminded Council that:

> we'd like to pursue…having an interactive session at the end (just prior to the business[s] meeting) that would be similar to what was done at the first conference in Texas….we're considering having a regular roundta-ble session of scholarly dialogues that might stimulate thinking among participants before meeting at the last Town Hall to consider together "where we are" five years after the Turning Point of the first annual C&P meeting (or however we'd like to frame it). At the Town Hall we would like to have the "founders" of C&P in an interactive dialogue with the general conference participants – a conversation that would be an ap-propriate ending to the fifth annual conference. (Allen, 2009, p. 6)

Just as Schutz (2001) asserts that Dewey envisioned schools as places where participants were engaged in "a continual process of democratic joint inquiry, [where participants become] a planning society that collaboratively adjusted itself and its shared goals to a constantly environment, aiming al-ways to deepen the possibilities for actualizing individual capacities in the midst of collective efforts" (p. 274), the C&P group sought to create such a community. As evidenced by the multiple topics explored over the past nine years, the Town Hall became a place of joint inquiry for the commu-nity: the first town hall in 2000 was about the field itself and was called "Small Gatherings, Shifting Conditions, and communities of Discourse," and then in 2004, we offered a celebration of the thirty-fifth anniversary of Schwab's *The Practical*; a second town hall that year was an inquiry into the death of curriculum studies. The next year in 2005 the town hall was fo-cused on how to build and support a public disciplinary community, fol-lowed by living out the C&P mission in 2006, and a senior scholars town hall was presented in 2008.

The founders of C&P agree with Dewey's (1929/1989) position that "de-mocracy… is a way of personal life…which provides a moral standard for personal conduct" and that curriculum settings should be designed to serve as *special* cultural sites of democratic living (p. 101). The annual conference with the democratic community of the town hall represents just such a site. As democratic educators, C&P concurs with Dewey that the curricular focus should be on providing students with democratic experiences in the here-and-now of their educational lives and not in some vague, promised future. Democratic educators are committed to providing students with the curricular experiences that will broaden their understanding of the personal and social responsibilities of democratic living; just as C&P attempts to provide attendees with curricular experiences at the conference, in green spaces such as in the town hall.

The premises supporting this argument are based upon several types of data, which support our contention that the C&P town hall represents a unique democratic space as an embryonic community in the way that Dewey envisioned. These data sources include a content analysis of more than nearly nine thousand postings of the Council discussion records of comments by Council members form 2000-2007 on a private YahooGroup list and on a Wiki used for Council business (Allen, 2009). A second source of data are the conference publications which include the programs, copies of the edited book of proceedings, past issues of the *Journal of Curriculum and Pedagogy* and other archival materials. A third data source includes interviews with five of the C&P founders who created the Town Hall concept as a democratic community building practice. Triangulation was completed through the extensive content analysis of both the descriptive data derived from the Yahoo and Wiki listserv postings on the town halls, and from the conference publications, along with the personal interviews with the founders, all of which provided a synthesis of information about how the guiding principles are lived through the conference and the town hall.

Conclusions and Significance of Study

Over the course of the past ten years, the Curriculum and Pedagogy Conference has diligently worked to create and protect green spaces as Jim Sears, the first Council chair reminded Council in 2001"we don't try to encroach on "green spaces" and "town-hall meetings" to accommodate proposals" (Allen, 2009, p. 2). As the center piece of this democratic community, new Council members have been enculturated into understanding this concept of the democratic community space either by their yearly attendance at the conference or through the open discussion in the town hall planning and as Council members interact with each other on the electronic bulletin boards.

That is not to say that new Council members will always approach the planning of town halls with a clear knowledge or understanding about its history and importance to the values and guiding principles of the conference. This happened in 2009 when a new Council member wrote "I think we need to have a keynote in the formal sense of the word—not just a proposal/paper—I think this will help to draw folks in and in all honesty, I think we need something "flashy and sexy" (Allen, 2009, p. 12). A fellow Council member offered a cautionary reply:

> The community of scholars, forged in a space that offers voice & equity of recognition to graduate students, senior scholars and emerging scholars alike has been our hallmark for 10 years. Look at the wonderful senior scholars who attend C&P every year and who participate humbly and without fanfare... to change direction now would threaten the organization, itself, I think. (Allen, 2009, p. 12)

The creation of the Curriculum and Pedagogy Conference in 2000 was recognized as a turning point in the contemporary curriculum studies (Marshall et al., 2007). Along with other small conferences such as the American Association of Teaching and Curriculum (AATC) and the American Association for the Advancement of Curriculum Studies (AAACS), the Curriculum and Pedagogy Group offers a" hybridity of practice" (Marshall et al., p. 241) that is aimed at transforming the work of both practitioners and curriculum workers. What differentiates C&P from these other small conferences is the town hall space.

By emphatically rejecting the simplistic, standardized "keynote—star speaker" that dominates most large and small conferences in today's educational settings, C&P has sought to encourage complicated conversations across the conference and in the town hall where the meaning of democratic spaces and practices could be examined. In seeking to create this type of community in a unique democratic setting such as the town hall, the founders have created spaces for both opposition and connection where power and knowledge are challenged (Cary, 2004) and where new habits of mind can be experienced and created. Thus, the C&P Town Hall as a democratic space and its importance to the guiding principles upon which C&P was founded are representative of how the founders used the Deweyian concept of critical pragmatism to craft an embryonic community whereby new habits of mind and practice could be developed to disrupt old patterns and customs of conferences.

References

Allen, L. A. (2009). *The evolution of the C&P town hall, 2000-2008*. Paper presented at the 2009 annual Curriculum and Pedagogy Conference, Decatur, GA.

Allen, L. A. (2006). Silenced sisters: Dewey's disciples in a conservative new South, 1900-1940. *Journal of the Gilded Age and Progressive Era, 5*(2), 119-137.

Allen, L. A., Brooks, N., Marshall, D, Schubert, W., & Sears, J. (2000, November). Panelist: *Small gatherings, shifting coalitions and communities of discourse: Ongoing renovations to contemporary curriculum studies.* Conference on Curriculum and Pedagogy, Austin, TX.

Cary, L. (2004). Creating other oppositional spaces in curriculum studies. *Journal of Curriculum and Pedagogy 1*(1), 35-37.

Curriculum and Pedagogy Conference Programs (2000, 2001, 2002, 2003, 2004, 2005, 2006, 2007, 2008). Author's personal copies.

Dewey, J. (1932). The moral self. In L. A. Hickman & T. M. Alexander. (1998) *The essential Dewey*, Volume 2: Ethics, logic, psychology (pp. 341-354). Bloomington, IN: Indiana University Press.

Dewey, J. (1999). *Individualism old and new.* Amherst, NY: Prometheus Books. (Original work published 1929)

Marshall, J. D., Sears, J. T., Allen, L. A., Roberts, P., & Schubert, W. H. (2007). *Turning points in curriculum: A contemporary American memoir* (2nd ed.). Upper Saddle River, NJ: Prentice Hall.

Pinar, W. F., Reynolds, W. M., Slattery, P., & Taubman, P. M. (1995). *Understanding curriculum: An introduction to the study of historical and contemporary curriculum discourses.* New York: Peter Lang.

Rohmann, C. (1999). *A world of ideas: A dictionary of theories, concepts, beliefs and thinkers.* New York: Ballantine Books.

Zilversmit. A. (1993). *Changing schools: Progressive education theory and practice, 1930-1960.* Chicago: University of Chicago Press.

Whither Democratic Educational Leadership? On Questions of Institutionalization and Hypergovernability within Curriculum Studies

MICHAEL P. O'MALLEY AND ISRAEL AGUILAR
Texas State University—San Marcos

We find a sense of welcome invitation in this opportunity to reflect on the Curriculum and Pedagogy Group's mission, to consider a shared ground on which we stand even as landscapes shift continuously. We contribute our perspectives to the many voices across multiple venues (books, journal articles, chapters, conference papers at and beyond C&P, performances, town halls, calls for proposals, symposia, formal and informal discussions, emails) that probe, advance, contest, argue, and imagine possibilities for this group of educators, scholars, activists, and artists traveling in some way together, if only for a time. So, whither the ethical and political project of creating synergy and dissensus out of the "lines according to which boundaries and passages are constructed, according to which they are conceivable and modifiable" (Rancière, 2010, p. 218), amongst disciplined curriculum studies, critical pedagogy, and democratic educational leadership?

One of us has already argued elsewhere with Louise Allen that the curriculum-leadership bifurcation which permeates organizational structures across educational institutions from pre-K through academe more readily serves the interests of academics and P-12 educators seeking to build expertise and reputation in narrowly delineated disciplines or roles, academic units within universities that benefit from territorialized pathways to student matriculation, and a neoliberal corporatization of the academy that perceives knowledge as a discrete product to be distributed via the economic engines of capitalism (O'Malley & Allen, 2009). Locating such within the philosophical investments of modernity, we advocated engaging queer and postcolonial theoretical perspectives to construct an integrated curriculum leadership imaginary that transgresses modern mechanisms of standardization while creating through lines towards education understood as participatory, democratic, and communal experience. It is these last and in some sense eschatological questions of participation, democracy, and community that we (Michael and Israel) take up here.

To the degree that the Curriculum and Pedagogy Group's genesis and early mission articulation posed radical commitments to democratic spaces and public moral leadership through dialogue and action, the group offers a community of living experience through which we might understand "lines according to which boundaries and passages are constructed." The immediately pressing question from our perspective lies in the arena of institutionalization and the lines that it generates. That is, what restratifications of the eruptive line of flight occur as an original yet partial charism of democracy becomes contextualized within the institutional mechanisms that evolve to guarantee the functioning of the organization, and in regards to various subjectivities positioned differently in relation to those institutional structures? We consider the most valuable and subversive line of the C&P By-Laws to be the annotation that "the membership at the Annual Meeting … as a body of the whole, is the sole and final decision-making body of this organization" (Curriculum & Pedagogy Group, 2005, para. 5.c.2). Reading this bold stance against constraints of representative democracy as hyperbolic rhetoric, an increased possibility if the mission and by-laws are read ahistorically, would likely involve a greater degree of eisegesis than by-laws commonly invite. Recognizing it as deliberative, on the other hand, forwards the emphasis on the membership as the "sole" decision making body as indicative of an immediate tension with every necessary decision the Council makes in its role of stewarding the organization.

We argue that this tension urges us as a group to take seriously the need to wisely limit expectations regarding Council's role as an oversight body, arbiter of initiatives, measure for transparency, or primary location for democratic deliberation. This tension calls for reimagining mental models that might place the Council in the center of the organization, or conceptualize it as the site of decisions for and about the community that is Curriculum and Pedagogy. The converse to this reimagining would appear to us to be movement in the direction of hypergovernability, which places disproportionate emphasis on the functioning of democratic institutions and which positions a society's members as beneficiaries of such institutions rather than as deliberative actors in their own right (Cuadra, 2007). Within a logic of hypergovernability, Council would be a democratic and benevolent institution that makes subtle or explicit decisions about what can or cannot be said, how, and by whom in terms of expressing the vision, voice, priorities, or experience of the living community that is the Curriculum and Pedagogy Group. Members, within this dynamic, are enticed to become beneficiaries of Council's democratic leadership in ways that involve ceding the capacity to be deliberative actors making public decisions about participation, democracy, and community.

Pragmatically, there is an admitted impossibility to reserving all decisions to the membership convened in the Annual Meeting. Our suggestion within this governance dilemma is to embrace the principle of subsidiarity, meaning that decisions that do not clearly need to be made by Council ought not to be made by Council. Subsidiarity calls for wisdom in distinguishing Council decisions necessary to facilitate and nurture the work of the organization throughout the year from those that substantively affect the organization as a whole (including vision, priorities, and resource allocation) that ought to be taken up by the membership, leaving the wide remainder to the joyful, contentious, divergent play among many deliberative, participatory actors. Walking across boundaries of institutionalization and hypergovernability and through passages of dissensus and subsidiarity, consistently seeking awareness of our own implication in exclusion and circulations of power (Pinar, 2009), the C&P community can be a site for working out democratic educational leadership that is distinct from the representative structures we have inherited within a larger public sphere, and become a resource for Curriculum Studies organizations, schools, and educational sites seeking to reimagine participatory leadership.

References

Cuadra, F. M. de la. (2007). Conflicto social, hipergobernabilidad y participación ciudadana: Unanálisis de la "revolución de los pingüinos". *Polis, Revista de la Universidad Bolivariana*, 5(16), 1-32.

Curriculum and Pedagogy Group. (2005, June 28). *By-Laws*. Retrieved from: http://www.curriculumandpedagogy.org/By-Laws.html

O'Malley, M. P., & Allen, L. A. (2009). Curriculum leadership as a democratic project: The case for reconfiguring educational structures. In J. Burdick, J. A. Sandlin, & T. Daspit (Eds.), *Complicated conversations and confirmed commitments: Revitalizing education for democracy* (pp. 229-251). Troy, NY: Educator's International Press.

Pinar, W. F. (2009). The unaddressed 'I' of ideology critique. *Power and education, 1*(2), 189-200.

Rancière, J. (2010). *Dissensus: On politics and aesthetics* (S. Corcoran, Ed. & Trans.). London: Continuum.

Gravity and Grace in Curriculum Studies

NANCY J. BROOKS
Ball State University

It is possible that we are living in an era more amenable to the return of holistic, democratically oriented curriculum work than any time since the pre-Sputnik era. The post-Sputnik transfer of responsibility for curriculum planning into the hands of disciplinary scholars constituted the abandonment of big-picture curriculum thinking and enshrined a piecemeal, technocratic approach to curriculum development. The new curriculum "experts" gave little attention to whether their innovations were consistent with one another or fostered common purposes.

Fifty years later it appears that much remains the same, with our current emphasis on curriculum as content standards and the definition of teachers (by some reformers) as primarily subject area experts. In spite of this, the social, economic, and political tumult of a now broadly recognized transition to a post-industrial age has opened a space for discussion of the need for new educational structures. In addition, political pressures have inspired even the most practical minded educators to search for new curricular arrangements. Most current experiments (e.g., New Tech High and Project Lead the Way) are still driven by the social efficiency priorities of our age, but I am seeing a new curiosity in my graduate students and a greater openness to exploring varieties of curriculum possibilities.

However slim it may seem to some, these current conditions represent an opportunity for us to advance—as Jim Henderson has phrased it in the opening chapter—"the synergistic relationship between disciplined curriculum studies, critical pedagogy and democratic educational leadership." C&P was established as a space for such opportunities to be initiated, explored, sculpted, and critiqued. While we have not been entirely ineffective, I believe we all hoped that we might see more fruit from our labors after a decade of work.

Therefore, my response to the prompt for this piece has been to consider the obstacles that prevent us from taking advantage of current favorable conditions to enact C&P's original intention of overcoming predominant bifurcations of theory/practice, academy/P-12, curriculum/pedagogy. Because we labor in difficult times, I can imagine that if the C&P Group were to conduct an honest brainstorming session we could produce quite an impressive list of contributing factors to our difficulty. I will focus upon just one: the considerable and continuing distance between the horizons of curriculum workers in schools and those in the academy. A central goal of C&P has been the dissolution of this bifurcation in order to allow for a fusion of curriculum workers' horizons and the release of a generative synergy; however, the divide persists.

In defense of our feeble results, neither the academy nor the P-12 environment encourage a deepening of personal understanding, in the sense of understanding one's personal horizons in comparison with any Other's. In schools the unrelenting focus is on our ability to produce "achievement" in the form of test scores. In the academy we are driven to conquer specific intellectual territory in a competitive arena, in order to prove its worth. As a result we all, as C&P members, come together from culturally different but similarly high pressured contexts, determined to overcome what dominates our worlds.

Simone Weil would counsel us, however, that two forces rule the universe: gravity and grace. Gravity is the imperative and the central law of this world. It is the force that institutionalizes and animates our individual and collective efforts to exercise power over all of which we are capable, to strive toward success and legitimacy. It is the natural environment within which most of us dwell in this age of accountability. When we turn our attention to the C&P project, it is highly likely that we continue to be animated by this default motivation, in spite of the fact that it is at odds with core C&P values and "disciplined, open-minded, open-hearted dialogue" (from Henderson's introduction).

Weil (1952) proposed that we escape the demands of gravity only through grace, which she associates with right relationships: "We have to see things in right relationship and ourselves, including the purposes we bear within us, as one of the terms of that relationship" (p. 96). This entails the *decreating* of self, an unconditional consent to be nothing: "We can offer nothing short of ourselves. Otherwise, what we term our offering is merely a label under which the 'I' is compensated" (p. 21). Significantly, this is not accomplished by will (by whipping the self into shape), but by grace, which comes from beyond ourselves, from that pure goodness, which Weil calls God: "It penetrates into our souls as a drop of water makes its way though geological strata without affecting their structure and it waits in silence until we consent to become God again" (p. 21).

Gravity stops the flow of life in order to comprehend, institutionalize, and make use of it. But, ironically, as soon as we grasp life, we overcome it. Through grace, however, we have the opportunity to enact something similar to Badiou's ethical fidelity by surrendering what we "know" in order to allow the life of each unique individual to be animated "internally by everything of which it is capable" (Badiou, 2003, p. 103).

If Weil is correct, C&P's success will depend upon our ability to surrender ways of being that are deeply engrained. It will also require us to be brutally honest in answering the questions that Henderson poses in the introduction to these essays regarding the driving force behind C&P and who it benefits. This is a daunting task. Realizing that we are humans influencing other human beings and that we often error in delivering on our promised results, we would do well to attend to Huebner's (1966) exhortation on the ethical values of promise and forgiveness:

> Forgiveness unties man from the past that he may be free to contribute to new creation....As long as man is finite, promise must be accompanied by the possibility of forgiveness, otherwise only the old, the known, the tried and tested will be evoked (p. 23).

References

Badiou, A. (2003). *Saint Paul: The foundation of universalism* (R. Brassier, Trans.). Stanford, CA: Stanford University Press.

Huebner, D. E. (1966). Curriculum as a field of study. In H. Robinson (Ed.), *Precedents and promise in the curriculum field* (pp. 94-112). New York: Teachers College Press.

Weil, S. (1952). *Gravity and grace* (A. Wills, Trans.). Lincoln: University of Nebraska Press.

Praxis, Space, and Revolution or I Just Can't Be (Queer)

FRANCIS S. BROADWAY
The University of Akron

A society fashioned in harmony with the American democratic tradition would ... finally be prepared as a last resort, in either the defense or the realization of this purpose, to follow the method of revolution (Counts, 1932/1978, p. 38).

Queer theory posits to queer itself. By definition, to queer means that there is no "G-d saw all that he had made, and it was very good" (Gen 1:31 NIV), but rather there is a rupture of the critical understanding of the normalized (hegemonic) natural. Queer cannot be perceived as normalized natural. Thus, the Curriculum and Pedagogy Group's mission (**C&P mission),** in its actions and reflections, inhibits queer (v.) by reforming a space for curriculum and pedagogy into a place for curriculum and pedagogy rather than transforming space. **C&P mission** has impelled a multitude of rebellions in the American [sic] tradition, but not the revolution that is a sufficient and necessary condition of democracy.

A frontier—awaiting ... and inviting (Dewey, 1936/1987, p. 168)

[Place is] "a context [for] the development of a sense of self and sense of being in the world" (Whitlock, 2007, p. 2).

In the clauses such as: "space where work can be shared, valued and disseminated" and "the conference creates democratic spaces", the C&P mission explicate space. From the outset, the connotation of space necessitates unknowing and, if anything, a search for more unknowing rather than a search for knowing or its more complicated destination, understanding. Thus, **C&P mission**, in order to have an identity or be a difference, becomes a place or something knowable. The mission statement, through colorings that obviate space by constructing boundaries that are the markers of place, invites the destruction of space through the power of naming. In the terms of space, to name is to limit such that space becomes bounded and circumscribed—place. Could space be limitless and unknown and at the same time known and constrained? The contradiction or paradox of the (un)bound and the (un)known queers space. Space cannot exist, but what can exist is an I.

As I clamor for being someone or defined by others, I search for boundaries that are ambiguous and fluid and yet, are boundaries nevertheless. These boundaries give me "a sense of self and a sense of being in the world" (Whitlock, 2007, p. 2) or these boundaries are (my) place. Instead of shedding these boundaries, I explore how best to wrap myself into boundaries so that I am (acceptable and knowable). These boundaries are political, sexual, raced, cultural, historical, gendered, economical, (auto)biographic, performative, or whatever might cause me to be (named). Hence, rather than opening space, the necessity to be an I has created a place named the Curriculum and Pedagogy Group or the *Journal of Curriculum and Pedagogy*. As the **C&P mission** creates "no place like home" for curriculum and pedagogy, place salvages and normalizes naturally the stranger—the "I am" without identity—in terra incognita.

> Liberation is a praxis: the action and reflection of men and women upon their world in order to transform it (Freire, 1970/2000, p. 79).

To create a place for curriculum and pedagogy, reflection or actions of reflection must occur; however space, as queer, is praxis. The C&P mission facilitates reflection (n.) and reflection (v.) to know the world of school. Whereas a space for curriculum and pedagogy invites revolutionary action for men and women to understand via transforming that place called school (n.) to a space called education (v.) that is both queer, because it "offers the possibility, but does not in itself effect, the destabilization of categories" (Phelan, 2001, p. 111), and strange, as it "is not just 'not like us,'...but may 'pretend' to be like us" (p. 31).

Furthermore, place, as the appellation of the **C&P mission**, reflectively calls for a cornucopia of (un)silenced voices. This changing of the voices of the oppressed does not eliminate the oppressed and the oppressor. These voices, (un)silenced and of which one is mine, do not know how to act differently, oppressionless. Thus, the plea for the (un)silencing of the oppressed through reflection prompts creation of and rebellion for a new voice, a new oppressor.

Thus, the action of **C&P mission**, in terms of making students successful, makes students and us school folks, using Luhmann's (1998) word, "palatable" for the schools. The **C&P mission** creates a place called school where one follows and finds the American [sic] Dream (Levine & Scheiver, 2010) albeit the plutocratic United States is the embodiment of a plantation with masters and slaves including the overseers—often us classroom teachers, school administrators, curriculum workers, teacher educators, etc.—who desire to be the oppressed, but are oppressors. To transform school is to create a revolutionary frontier space that liberates and educates. In other words, the democratic liberation space called education for

- a White male nearing 30 years of age who is the son of a father who is a self-employed small businessman and for which two of his three brothers, not him, have completed high school; did not complete high school; lives with his parents; unmarried; the sire of three children from two women for which two children live in another part of a state in which he resides and one near his father's home; and unemployed and not attending school, now, still, unemployed after leaving his last two jobs after three days on the job; and

- Levine and Scheiver's (2010) Leo, now dead;

must engender, propagate, and invent, in Steiner's words (2003), an awakening of the human powers within the person; dreaming beyond one's own dreams; loving "that which one loves; [and] to make of one's inward present their future" (p. 183-184).

Thus, as the words of identity, difference, justice, equity, peace, and political, economic, spiritual (auto)biographical, and historical consciousness that are gendered, sexual, raced, and cultured are spoken, the rebellion lead by **C&P mission** is the emperor's new clothes. To acknowledge a rebellion is occurring rather than a revolution is to forego queer (v.) and "as an incomplete being in a sea of possibility" (Phelan, 2001, p. 129), to meet the enemy and it is I.

References

Counts, G. S. (1932/1978). *Dare the school build a new social order.* Carbondale: Il: Southern Illinois University Press.

Dewey, J. (1936/1987). Education and new social ideals. In Boydston, J. A. (Ed.), *John Dewey: The later works, 1925–1953,* (Volume 11, pp. 167–180). Carbondale, IL: Southern Illinois University Press.

Freire, P. (1970/2000). *Pedagogy of the oppressed* (30th Anniversary ed.). New York: Continuum.

Levine, A., & Scheiver, L. (2010). *Unequal Fortunes: Snapshots from the South Bronx.* New York, NY: Teachers College Press

Luhmann, S. (1998). Queering/querying pedagogy? Or, pedagogy is a pretty queer thing. In W. F. Pinar (Ed.), *Queer Theory in Education* (pp. 141- 155). Mahwah, NJ: Lawrence Erlbaum Associates.

Phelan, S. (2001). *Sexual strangers: Gay, lesbians, and dilemmas of citizenship.* Philadelphia, PA: Temple University Press.

Steiner, G. (2003). *Lessons of the masters.* Cambridge, MA: Harvard University Press.

Whitlock, R. U. (2007). *This corner of Canaan: Curriculum studies of place & the reconstruction of the South.* New York: Peter Lang Publishing.

KENT DEN HEYER
University of Alberta

Urban Love Story

A boy loved a girl who lived on the 40th floor
of a crumbling old building.
The space between the top of her balustrade
and the bottom of the floor above was
five or six feet,
maybe seven on a sunny day.
So the boy ties up rocks of twenty with "I love you" notes
because his father told him, and I think rightly so,
"If you are going to tell someone you love them, let them know."
Full moon, night of electric blue forever
threatening to disrupt the balance between night and day
our hero showed up below her 40th floor
and he tossed and he tossed.
Not once did he hit between the seven feet,
actually six,
it was not a sunny day.
Slowly people looked out of their windows cracked
to see who had interrupted pre-packaged conceptions
of the colour blue and spied
the poor boy looking into his empty hands.
They came down from their broken windows
and stood with him through the night.
While he did not break through the window of his love
I hear many others are still friends today…

Quanta viable

Evaporation, condensation, drips and drops
Between stars and I, drips drop dreams
Potential begets being in supreme possibility
virtual almosts, spaces that scream
into new born nexus points
our inter-stellar dreams.

I can make no claim to poetry, but I did attempt to write two poems. They express my response both to the question of an ethical fidelity to any mission, and, the infinite here in which such takes place. Not adept at the art, I tried to engage in something new and strange for me for which I lack comfort or indeed grace. Yet, in this novice attempt, I have tried to enact a task being advanced in this book — to begin.

Engaging Dissensus: Selected Principles and Reflections

THOMAS E. KELLY
John Carroll University

Platform Planks

I want to take up Jim Henderson's prompt from the following four platform planks:

> This book and Jim's related work with Kathleen Keeson *(Curriculum Wisdom)* and Rosie Gornik *(Transformative Curriculum Leadership, 3ʳᵈ edition)* represent a scholarly, systematic, and compelling vision of priority goals, artistries, understandings, and challenges related to educating in/for democratic living.

> Immanent critique is imperative, for all. Given unceasing human fallibility and the often indeterminate relationship between means and ends, immanent critique essentially represents a non-negotiable commitment to integrity. Compatible with Jim's introductory chapter explication, I define immanent critique as the twin act of: a) analyzing the degree to which individuals and organizations walk their own talk, and b) adjusting consciousness and conduct, policies and practices to achieve their more faithful and noble congruence. At its best, conscientious immanent critique is embraced from within, en-

couraged from outside (e.g. through 'critical friends') and done systematically and routinely.

Conscientious immanent critique recognizes that individuals, culture, history and social structures, while not necessarily symmetrical in influence, are mutually constitutive and mutually determining. Hence, robust analyses and adjustments associated with immanent critique, reflecting a fundamental Deweyian commitment to "eschew reductive and dualistic explanations," seek to approach integrity by accounting for these complex interactions.

Following Ranciere (2010), dissensus is a central, inescapable dynamic in a democracy. It *can* be generative of considerable personal, social, and structural disequilibrium which in turn can, in complex and confounding ways, reinforce prejudice, dampen generosity, suppress self-interrogation, intensify systemic inequality, and constrict the commitment to sustaining engagement across and through difference; an engagement upon which a thriving participatory democracy pivotally depends. Further, when magnified by distorting hyperbole and polarizing partisanship associated with toxic asymmetries of power, dissensus can assume a particularly diabolical character: to disagree is to defeat, to disapprove, to disrespect, to demean, to discount, to dehumanize, to demonize.

Fortunately, dissensus need not be reduced to threat and imposition. It can be, indeed must be, also realistically addressed as opportunity and challenge. Overall, constructively addressing various forms of dissensus involves both education and political struggle.

Caveats

While political analysis and struggle are profoundly important, my remarks below primarily focus on educational efforts drawn from my professional experience in the context of interpersonal dissensus. Additionally, in terms of immanent critique, my comments are intended to offer general perspectives for consideration rather than specific critiques targeting particular initiatives and practices Jim and his colleagues and/or the C&P Group should or should not pursue.

Teasing and Toughing Out, Then Trying to Transcend and Twine Tenacious Tensions

In a thought exercise during a recent graduate seminar I taught, one that focused on democracy, conflict and controversy in education, students unanimously arrived at two determinations: 1) there is never a time when schools and teachers are not teaching values; and 2) there were no values that they could identify that simultaneously met three conditions: a) they were unequivocally desirable; b) they were unambiguous; c) they were un-controversial. Privacy, helping others, discipline, success, honor, respect, the golden rule—each candidate, under scrutiny, failed the test.

Through that course, and the curriculum of my life, I have come to be impressed that dissensus is ubiquitous, unavoidable, unsettling... and yet, exceptionally educative. It lives below and above the surface, in ways sub-dued and subtle, vital, and volcanic. In an era of instant information and shout sensationalism, the facts and perspectives we encounter are certainly not always reliable or well-reasoned. However, despite any distortions and defamations, the interpretative frame and sense of ethical fidelity I strive to embrace within dissensus are grounded in the dignifying not dismissive or demeaning belief that *reasonable* people can and do disagree about a myriad of interrelated, complex factual, definitional and value issues. I believe the dissensus around the pursuit of this book instantiates this perspective.

Thus, in my various inquiries into matters of truth, meaning, and moral-ity, I aspire to faithfully walk my own talk as inquisitive, respectful learner and teacher by experiencing and insuring a 'best case fair hearing' for com-peting perspectives, embracing contraries through the creative arts of dis-cussion facilitation (Kelly, 2001) and through the arts of deliberation and imagination that Elbow (1986) terms methodological believing (MB) and methodological doubting (MD). These yin and yang practices represent complementary, disciplined moments in examining the validity and value of standpoints under study. In the pursuit of understanding not necessarily agreement, the inquirer alternately foregrounds a generous, empathic inter-pretative stance toward presented ideas (MB) and a respectful but skeptical scrutiny of the assertions, assumptions and implications of these ideas (MD). MB seeks to deliberately counteract any tendency toward pejora-tive, premature rejection while MD seeks to offset gullible, inconsiderate approval (Kelly, 2005). At its best, this process critically analyses what Muwakkil (2010) decries as the paralyzing "faux symmetry of on-the-other-hand 'objectivity'" (p. 20).

The gold standard I use for judging the fluent integration of competing perspectives is the multiple Oscar nomination. Can I and my disputants, colleagues and students portray the targeted worldview of divergent, op-positional others in such an empathic, nuanced manner as to figuratively earn an Oscar endorsement for the deep representation of the inhabited perspectives? While never guaranteed, it is my hypothesis that activity which aspires and capacitates toward this ideal can nurture understandings and dispositions that over time expand the problem solving possibilities for honoring and harmonizing contesting needs, and thus transcending obsta-cles, once seen as insurmountable.

Honing and Harnessing a Humbling Chutzpah.

That reconciliation of dissensus in particular cases *can* happen with assis-tance from the imaginative/deliberative arts clearly does not mean that it *will* happen in all cases. Nor is the dignifying sensitivity toward self and others that I am enthusiastically associating with these arts meant to translate into a reductionist, relativist stance regarding the substantive merits of distinct positions. That is, not all viewpoints are equally valid. By virtue of their clarity, coherence, comprehensiveness, factual credibility, integration of antagonistic worldviews and differentiated attunement with the subaltern, some perspectives are decidedly better, more compelling, more inclusive, more just than competing positions. Such positions deserve to be taken up with passionate righteousness and all the political acumen and strategic re-sourcefulness one can muster...overridingly including the regulating recog-nition of a set of transcendent first principles: that Gandhi trumps Machiavelli, that process is substance, that manner is message, that means to noble ends should themselves be noble, that deviations from this nobility require rigorous 'burden of proof' justifications, that 'for all' fidelity to righteous causes, waged by the inescapably fallible, compels ardent <u>and</u> humble advocacy, sustained commitment <u>and</u> open-minded self critique, cogent objections to the dehumanization of others <u>and</u> their authoritative expression in non-dehumanizing terms and tenor.

Over the years, for both students, schools and self, I have sought to en-hance what might be called the arts of conflict negotiation, drawing on and adapting principles discussed in the widely acclaimed text, *Getting to yes: Negotiating agreement without giving in* (1991). In my experience, as individu-als/disputants learn to separate the person from the problem, reframe prob-lematic conduct as expressions of unmet needs, listen reflectively, focus on interests not positions, avoid confounding means and ends, explicitly con-firm common interests, explore options for mutual gain, look to embrace a WIN-WIN mentality, insist on using more 'objective' criteria of adjudication (laws, rules, contracted agreements) and seek to collaboratively agree on standards of fairness, what substantially increases is their willingness and capacity to confront conflict, to see the potential for synthesis, reconciliation and mutual benefit and to work toward these goals. Significantly, these particular arts eschew both aggressive imposition and timid self-sacrifice, encouraging in their stead a marvelous middle passage characterized by steely strength in advocating one's interests <u>and</u> empathic attunement to the interests of others, a principled firmness <u>and</u> resourceful flexibility.

Of course, these arts of conflict negotiation fall capaciously short of being a panacea. For a host of interlaced intrapersonal/unconscious, interpersonal, cultural and social-systemic reasons, individuals may perceive their priority interests to be irreconcilable and thus 'getting to yes' remains elusive. Additionally, while these arts of negotiation are applicable in all human interactions, challenges we face in the curriculum field demand mobilizing practical insights and progressive impact on the local, national and international levels in the spheres of schools, business organizations, communities, media and policy legislation. In this effort, expanding our scope and drawing on the insights of Michael Fullan, Chris Argyris, Saul Alinsky, and Eric Alterman among a host of others would seem vital. As the final chapter in this book manifests, Jim, Rosie, and their colleagues have their sights set on particular dimensions of systemic change as they enact the lead learner role of facilitating professional learning communities and encouraging public intellectual activity.

Debriefing Dialogic Dynamics: Principles & Probes to Ponder

I close with a set of questions meant to reflect many of the ideas I have articulated in this brief commentary. The questions are intended to serve as a sort of 'debriefing rubric' that individuals might use in assessing the fidelity to decent and educative democratic dialogue in the context of dissensus. Ideally, if not always practical, disputants will set aside time to collaboratively discuss these and/or related questions.

- Where and why do you think we significantly agree and disagree?

- What new perspectives and previous standpoints (beliefs, values, assumptions) do we each want to further consider?

- How do we assess the extent to which we spoke to each other with an optimal blend of candor <u>and</u> sensitivity, generosity <u>and</u>

challenge? Where there moments when we felt unheard or dismissed?

- Put differently, what are we respectively proud about and what refinements are needed in terms of how we talked to/with/at each other?

- Are there any other feelings and/or provisional effects from our conversation--yet undisclosed--that would be helpful, honest and/or honorable to share at this time?

- Do we want to continue this conversation? Why? Why not? If yes, when?

References

Elbow, P. (1986). *Embracing contraries: Explorations in learning and teaching.* New York: Oxford University Press.

Fisher, R., Ury, W., & Patton, B. (1991). *Getting to yes: Negotiating agreement without giving in.* Cambridge: Harvard University Press.

Kelly, T. (2001). *Discussing controversial issues: Four perspectives on the teacher's role.* In W. Hare & J. Portelli (Eds.) *Philosophy of education: Introductory readings* (3rd ed., pp. 221-242). Calgary: Detselig Enterprises, Ltd.

Kelly, T. (2005). Transcending false dichotomies: The dynamics of doubt and certainty. In D. A. Breault & R. Breault (Eds.), *Experiencing Dewey: Insights for today's classroom* (pp. 73-76). Indianapolis: Kappa Delta Phi.

Henderson, J. G., & Gornik, R. (2006). *Transformative curriculum leadership* (3rd ed.). Upper Saddle River, NJ: Prentice Hall.

Henderson, J. G., & Kesson, K. (2003). *Curriculum wisdom: Educational decisions in democratic societies.* Upper Saddle River, NJ: Prentice Hall.

Muwakkil, S. (Aug. 30/Sept. 6, 2010). Reply to Eric Alterman's "Dabuki Democracy." *The Nation.* 20.

Ranciere, J. (2010). *Dissensus: On politics and aesthetics* (S. Corcoran, Ed. & Trans.). London: Continuum.

Wheels Have Been Set in Motion: Visions and Reflections

KRIS SLOAN
St. Edward's University

Visions

> *Guildenstern*: *Wheels have been set in motion*, and they have their own pace, to which we are....condemned. Each move is dictated by the previous one — that is the meaning of order. If we start being arbitrary it'll just be a shambles: at least, let us hope so. Because if we happened, just happened to discover, or even suspect, that our spontaneity was part of their order, we'd know that we were lost (Stoppard, 1967, p. 60)

Reflections

In trying to understand the C & P Conference project (hereafter, "C & P"), and my involvement in it, I frequently turn to the Shakespearean characters Rosencrantz and Guildenstern as re-imagined by Tom Stoppard (Stoppard, 1967).[1] In Shakespeare's play, *Hamlet* is visited by two friends, Rosencrantz and Guildenstern. These friends have come at the behest of Hamlet's mother, Queen Gertrude and his new stepfather, the newly crowned King *Uncle* Claudius. The Queen and the new King charged the two friends with the specific purpose of ascertaining what it is that *afflicts* poor Hamlet, and to help them cure or at least pacify this *affliction*. In the Shakespeare version, Rosencrantz and Guildenstern are but ancillary characters whose

---

[1] This has been an on-going project of mine, as well as a long-term collaboration with Ken den Heyer, who also contributed to this collection of responses. More on this on-going collaboration forthcoming.

roles are offered up as sacrificial lambs to demonstrate one of Hamlet's many contradictions. The Rosencrantz and Guildenstern of Stoppard's play, however, find themselves thrust into the center of a Shakespearean maelstrom filled with retribution, duplicity, ambition, loyalty, and ultimately fate.

Visions

After only a brief encounter, Rosencrantz and Guildenstern diagnose Hamlet's *affliction* with quick and comic precision:

> *Rosencrantz*: To sum up: your father, whom you love, dies, you are his heir, you come back to find that hardly was the corpse cold before his young brother popped onto this throne and into his sheets, thereby offending both legal and natural practice. Now why exactly (Hamlet) are you behaving in this extraordinary manner?
>
> *Guildenstern*: I *can't* imagine! (Pause.) But all that is well known, common property. Yet he sent for us. And we did come (Stoppard, 1967, p. 51).

The conundrum, of course, is that the Queen Mother and the King Uncle await this diagnosis as well as suggested remedies. The two friends know what *afflicts* Hamlet, but because of their place in the social and political order of an already reeling Denmark, they cannot say. The two friends fear the response a wider public naming of Hamlet's *affliction* would cause.

Reflections

In thinking carefully about Jim Henderson's prompt concerning the **ethical fidelity** of C & P many questions come to mind. First, can a summarization of a mission statement, in fact, two mission statements, adequately direct questions over the **ethical fidelity** of the current state of C & P? That is to say, does the 21-word summarization of the C & P/JCP mission statements offered in the introduction adequately capture the multilayered, 130+ word mission statement? Second, whenever questions arise over the overall quality of curriculum work and "disciplined" becomes the signifier of quality, I wonder how, or who draws the line between "undisciplined"/ "disciplined." Last, I have questions about what is meant by "democratic educational leadership," and how one might ascertain, or approach questions concerning the overall "democratic-ness" of a group such as C & P.

Visions

> *Rosencrantz*: I'm sorry I----What's the matter with you?
>
> *Guildenstern*: The scientific approach to the examination of phenomena is a defence against the pure emotion of fear. Keep tight hold and continue while there's time. ...(Stoppard, 1967, p. 17).

Reflections

In the Foreword of the edited collection from the first C & P Conference (Sloan & Sears, 2001), one strand of the origins narrative of the C & P project unwinds: "...*a unique confluence of events* brought together many kindred spirits in the formation of an exciting new conference" (Slattery, 2000, p. xii). From the very beginning of this project, there was an open prohibition of public conversations about specific, but important aspects of this *unique confluence of events*. Specifically prohibited were public conversations involving critiques directed at individuals or other small curriculum gatherings. Still however, these specific, even personal critiques, even grievances, helped structure the language that eventually formed significant planks of the C & P project mission statement: "...*The conference creates democratic spaces to advance public moral leadership in education through dialogue and action....*" The deployment of both "democratic spaces" and "public moral leadership" carry with them the *baggage* alluded to in "*a unique confluence of events.*"

Equally present and important in the origins narrative for C & P were notions of *transparency*. As I wrote in the introduction of the first edited proceedings, "Central to the idea of democratic community building was a collective belief among the conversation participants is the notion of transparency" (Sloan, 2001, p. xvii).

In his introductory chapter to this book, Jim Henderson directs some of his questions regarding the **ethical fidelity** of the C & P project at the group's governance practices. He worries that "too much emphasis on establishing a collective C&P identity might work against practicing the art of personal understanding, particularly with reference to undertaking creative initiatives." Later he adds, "Peer review is not automatically 'democratic.'" Here Jim identifies an interesting set of tensions between *democratic* practices and actions conducted under conditions of full *transparency*. That the C & P governance structure so adheres to the notion of transparency, perhaps even "peer review," cannot be understood outside of the context of C & P's origins narrative in general, and the *unique set of circumstances* that led to C & P.

When I look at the 130+ word mission statement adopted by C & P, I see specific language that calls for an opening up of spaces for a wide array of curriculum work from a wide array of curriculum workers: "*...a gathering of diverse individuals... where work can be shared, valued, and disseminated to a diverse audience committed to educational reform and social change.... characterized by its commitment to classroom teachers, school administrators and curriculum workers and in providing a venue for under-represented groups.*" Taken as a whole, the C & P mission statement represents a genuine effort to reach out, to be inclusive to a wide array of curriculum work. The mission statement calls out to curriculum workers who may not be engaged in *advancing the synergistic relationship between disciplined curriculum studies, critical pedagogy and democratic leadership* as it is understood, or outlined by Jim Henderson in both the introductory and concluding chapters.

Through my work in the mentoring strand, where early-career curriculum workers seek guidance and support, and through my frequent conversations with first-time attendees, I find the most common responses offered for attending usually approximate these aspects of the mission statement, "*....a gathering of diverse individuals seeking academic enrichment, social action, and professional engagement... an annual space where work can be shared, valued, and disseminated to a diverse audience committed to educational reform and social change...*"

Visions

Guildenstern: No. (*At footlights.*) What a fine persecution –to be kept intrigued without ever quite being enlightened….(*Pause.*). We've had no practice.

Rosencrantz: We could play questions.

Guildenstern: What good would that do?

Rosencrantz: Practice!

Guildenstern: Statement! One - love.

Rosencrantz: Cheating!

Guildenstern: How?

Rosencrantz: I hadn't started yet.

Guildenstern: Statement. Two - love.

Rosencrantz: Are you counting that?

Guildenstern: What?

Rosencrantz: Are you counting that?

Guildenstern: Foul! No repetitions. Three - love. First game to...

Rosencrantz: I'm not going to play if you're going to be like that (Stoppard, 1967, p. 41-42).

References

Slattery, P. (2001). Forward. In K. Sloan & J. T. Sears (Eds.), *Democratic curriculum theory and practice: Retrieving public spaces* (pp. xxi-xiv). Troy, NY: Educators International Press, Inc.

Sloan, K., & Sears, J. T. (Eds.). (2001). *Democratic curriculum theory and practice: Retrieving public spaces*. Troy, NY: Educators International Press, Inc.

Stoppard, T. (1967). *Rosencrantz and Guildenstern are dead*. New York: Grove Weidenfeld.

I'm No Maxine Greene, but That Doesn't Mean I Have to Abandon My Passion: Enacting My Vision of Ethical Fidelity

ANDREW GILBERT
The Evergreen State College

Maxine Greene has inspired thousands with her tremendous work spanning several decades. Personally, she has helped me to keep fighting in an unjust world and to continually push my own understanding for what it means to teach with passion and care.

She definitely has a clear vision for "ethical fidelity." However, there are precious few who can match her vision, grace and ability with expressing the beauty of teaching. In this respect, I'm no Maxine Greene. However, I've inspired a few really good teachers...I'm trying to start a revolution one teacher at a time, because that is what I can do. So I continue to be unconcerned with impact factors, acceptance rates, number of manuscript publications...my professional legacy will be the relationships that I have built with classroom teachers.

As teacher educators and curriculum workers we are charged with creating future teaching professionals who will enter the classroom and provide innovative, meaningful education in a time of escalating educational fascism. Thus, we set in motion a vision of balance between the reality of schooling and the possibility of its potential. This is my constant struggle with my own "ethical fidelity." K-12 teachers also struggle with similar notions of "ethical fidelity." Often for the classroom teacher, the balance is tipped away from progressive possibilities because they envision their university professors as unfettered by top down pressures of testing, large class sizes, lack of funds, and the like. Problematically, our research often portrays K-12 teacher deficiencies as opposed to the successes of their/our work. Often these critiques of teacher practice are decontextualized from the obvious shortcomings that permeate all levels of education. It could be argued that it is easier to point the finger at those who rarely fight back as opposed to careful introspection of our own practices. It is exactly these types of complicated conversations that teacher educators must engage in if we plan to push our work toward more humane, loving teaching in our schools and enact our "ethical fidelity."

I continue to struggle with my own role within teacher education. Why have I not more strongly contested decisions made at the state level, which do not represent the complexity of teaching and learning? More troubling is how I, on occasion, will enact institutionalized behavior that helps to sustain the traditional notion of schooling. Dewey (1997/1938) warns against this notion of the institutionalization of our actions, "Those who adhered to the established system needed merely a few fine-sounding words to justify their existing practices. The real work was done by habits which were so fixed as to be institutional" (p. 29). It can be argued that both teachers and teacher educators understand and enact these institutionalized roles. We are both working within structures that seemingly limit our freedom to question the status quo (tenure and promotion, state testing, packaged curricula, etc.). Within these limiting contexts, both K-12 teachers and their teacher educators engage in institutionalized behaviors. We are seeking these "few fine-sounding words," where teachers will ask for "what works," and "just tell me what to do on Monday morning." We need to hear one another. We need to begin by investigating our own glass houses and interrupt the same practices we are asking our teachers to engage in and realize we play a major role for the condition of schooling in the 21st century.

In my own quest toward "ethical fidelity," I have chosen to leave a university setting (where I was promoted and tenured) to join a small, public liberal arts college that better matches my ethical stance on preparing teachers. At my prior university, there existed a palpable notion of accepting the inevitability of top down assessment measures much like how the Wildebeest stops fighting when the Lion latches onto its neck. This troubled me deeply. I fought hard, but the fight was eroding my passion. My new context has rekindled my passion and strengthened my resolve to stay true to my core vision of "ethical fidelity." My current school does not utilize faculty rank, which fosters a more collaborative and supportive culture, where voices are valued more equally. Secondly, all classes are collaborative, integrated and team-taught, which helps to fuel new ventures and ideas between faculty. Lastly, our students are not graded in a typical A-F fashion rather they are provided narrative evaluations of their progress. I have found that this new environment allows me to pursue my vision of "ethical fidelity" because the structure of the institution allows me to engage with students in a far different manner. For example, I am better able to demonstrate to future elementary teachers how to integrate content across a broad range of ideas because I will have modeled being a generalist for them.

I am not suggesting that everyone must leave the tenure-track to remain true to his or her vision for teaching, but I would like to implore each of us to look closely at our own actions as professors of Education in the 21st century. Do we utilize deficit thinking when it comes to teachers? Do we challenge large-scale institutional structures in our work or do we leave it up to others? Are we doing everything we can within our own programs or just following the historical model within our own institutions? Our work towards "ethical fidelity" should reflect this and grow and change in response to the most immediate needs of teachers and children. I am asking each of us to reflect closely on our thoughts and actions and remind ourselves for why we chose to do this work. Most of us did not join the professorate solely to make tenure and promotion, or to accept the inevitability of poor curricular decisions by state and federal legislatures, rather we felt we could enact important change. I ask each of us to find that place within ourselves and pursue those goals. If we each revitalize those commitments we will be able to reach the democratic potential that exists within our schools, communities and society at large.

Reference

Dewey, J. (1997/1938). *Experience and education*. New York, NY: Touchstone.

Reflections from the Space In-Between

AUDREY DENTITH
University of Texas San Antonio

FREDRIKA HARPER
Cedarburg School District

We are teachers with careers that span decades, white women, of the same age, with advanced degrees in education and leadership positions in our field. We live in complex spaces and act out from within multiple subject positions in our current roles as practitioner, scholar, mothers, grandmothers, and, importantly, friends. We were both K-12 teachers before earning doctorates. Audrey was a K-12 teacher and part-time administrator before becoming a full time university faculty where she has held faculty appointments in curriculum and educational administration. Fredrika taught K-12, served as a principal for a number of years, and, is currently, a district-level curriculum director and adjunct professor.

Here, we reflect on our collective experience in C&P, one that has provided a space for us to explore subjectivities, deconstruct and reconstruct identities across the complex terrain of our professional (and personal) lives through language and playful deliberation (Bakhtin, 1981). In a space outside of the academy and K-12 administration, through our affiliation with the C&P group, we found and refashioned another, an in-between space, a social and political interstice that has offered refuge (from prevailing discourses in our 'home' organizations) and challenge in the forging of viable connections between the separate worlds of practitioners and academics.

Although language needs to be understood within processes that are partial and ever dynamic, it is the central means by which we articulate our experiences and give them meaning. Through language, we constitute our actions, thoughts, feelings and desires both individually and as collective beings (Bahktin, 1981; Hernandnez, 1997). This meaning-making process engaged in over our years of involvement in C&P, became central in the reconceptualization and transformation of our practice as educators. Situated as we were/are in institutions that are formulated around particular traditional (masculine) ideals in the discourses of educational administration, the in-between space nurtured by C&P facilitated new subjectivities that continue to shape our work in immeasurable ways.

Significantly, this work has been grounded in and around methods of curriculum theorizing, making authentic the notion that,

> the curriculum is not comprised of subjects, but of Subjects, of subjectivity. The running of the course is the building of the self, the lived experience of subjectivity. Autobiography is an architecture of the self, a self we create and embody as we read, write, speak and listen…[it] is a self we cannot be confident that we know, but it is always in motion, and in time, defined in part by where it is not, when it is not, what it is not (Pinar, 2004, p. 220 as quoted in Miller, 2004, p. 231).

C&P became for us, asite for the construction of our own autobiographies, one that emanated from the scholarly work in curriculum theory, and extended into our collaborative efforts to connect the work of K-12 schools with the academy.

We met each other in 2004 in a district-led initiative that focused on teachers' critical consciousnesses and curricular abilities in the context of rapidly changing demographics. The work illuminated common threads between us and a relationship evolved around our shared interests. Taking seriously the mission of the C&P group that speaks of desires to extend and connect curriculum work among academia, K-12 practice and across public spheres, we submitted our first co-authored paper to the annual C&P meeting in 2006 that was held in Balcone Springs, TX. We were energized by the interactive dialogue among members of the group, the town hall meetings, communal dining and retreat style of the conference. Thoughtful senior scholars and C&P founders warmly supported us and expressed genuine interest in our exploration.

Collaborations such as ours were less prevalent in C&P than we had anticipated. The wider embrace of perspectives and the purposeful inclusion of practitioners (although *invited*) were absent and such consideration was largely silent. The C&P group, like all entities committed to democratic processes in its declarations, can only achieve its goals to the extent that the inclusion of all those representing the membership are involved in the decision-making and values construction of the same (Young, 2000). In C&P, the language and practices of the academy prevail and attention to the everyday practices of practitioners are marginalized. It is an academically arranged organization that places the priorities (finishing dissertations, finding mentors, and getting published) of assistant professors and fulltime graduate students as paramount. The desire to support the relationship among practitioners and academics and extend curriculum theorizing into public sites, unfortunately, took a back seat to these priorities.

We encountered other obstacles, too, evident in the language and pre-sumptive practices of academics. While particular aspects of the publicly stated mission seemed to hold little personal significance for many members beyond their 'career' goals, our own deeply regarded sense of the 'rightness' of our own cause along with the gentle encouragement and example of many of the senior scholars, helped us to summon the tenacity to continue. This became our personal embodiment of the mission...to find the useful-ness in the relationship we saw as wildly valid but not wholly imagined within the group.

An in-between space had been established, a site where we could rigor-ously reflect on the symbiotic potential that exists across the diversity of our sites of practice. The aesthetics of that first conference with its provocative music, the drumming session, the exuberant sing-alongs, mixed in amongst academic talks and deep conversation was absolutely exhilarating. The wine, food, music, and an image of a C&P member, a woman, dancing freely dance in the grass around the pavilion as Eliza Gilkyson sang "Man of God", brought alive the experience of reflective thought with conscious encounter. It helped us to break through the natural worry and insecurities one experiences embarking on a new adventure. In the infusion of the art and the play we experienced the intensity of that political moment in time, sensing through forms of art those desires and perspectives that we all share as members of this particular field and of this movement in curriculum stud-ies. The unique culture and language initiated us into a new space and into new ways of seeing, being and hearing, feeling and moving (Greene, 2001), and we were quite affected by the relationships fashioned through these experiences.

The sometimes artificially separate and divisive lines between academia and school practice, do not reveal the potential that lays dormant in the in-between space. The logic of purposeful alliance is commonsensical. Over these past half dozen years, we've realized, through intense engagement, that dissent and difference can lead to insights. We're learning to neither defend or indict, but, instead to work toward the development of what Spivak (1993) names *critical intimacy*, an informed view that can emanate only from deliberation and an acknowledgment of the subjectivity of as-sumption and action, altered always by time, place, position and location. In the in-between space, we have confronted assumptions and worked to dis-rupt meanings, with degrees of intellectual courage new to us and well be-yond that which might be termed 'professional collaboration'. Indeed, it is akin to life work, itself (Miller, 2005).

References

Bakhtin, M. (1981).*The dialogic imagination* (C. Emerson & M. Holquist, Trans). Austin, TX: University of Texas Press.

Dewey, J. (1916/1980). Democracy and education. In J. A. Boydston (Ed.), *John Dewey: The middle works, 1899-1953,* (Volume 9, pp. 1-402). Carbonale, IL: Southern Illinois University Press.

Greene, M. (2001).*Variations on a blue guitar: The Lincoln Center Institute lectures on aesthetic education.* New York: Teachers College Press.

Hernandez. A. (1997). *Pedagogy, democracy, and feminism: Rethinking the public sphere.* Albany, NY: State University of New York Press.

Miller, J. (2005). *Sounds of silence breaking: Women, autobiography, curriculum.* New York: Peter Lang.

Pinar, W. (1994). *What is curriculum theory?* Mahwah, NJ: Lawrence Erlbaum.

Young, M. (2000). *Inclusion and democracy.* Oxford, UK: Oxford University Press.

It's Been a Long Time Since I've Worn that Sash: Tales of a Girl Scout Dropout

SHERI LEAFGREN
Miami University

"I watch what I do to see what I really believe." ~ *Sister Helen Prejean*

In 1964, only three short months after flying up from Brownies to Juniors, I quit Girl Scouts. I distinctly remember my mother's disappointment and my frustrated explanation: "All we ever do is *talk* about what we're *going* to do." Eight years later, in similar fashion, I stopped attending church after spending my high school age years attending two Sunday services plus two youth group meetings per week. In the case of leaving church, the word "hypocrites" came up several times in my explanation to my mother.

My tendency to experience catalytic disillusionment continues. I have left and been asked to leave other organizations and institutions—schools, teams, marriages, councils, professional groups—always following a struggle to reconcile the way I *thought* things would be with the way things were; always after what I perceived as betrayals—of being lied to.

Maybe I am too literal; perhaps my high school senior class poll was correct, and I am "most gullible" after all—but I when I listen to promises, read mission statements, and take to heart a shared vision, I *believe* them. When I decide to join in and take part, it is because I have invested heart and soul in those agreed-upon purposes and when I realize that perhaps those values do not guide the group's actions as I thought they would —that those involved seem not to be, as Maxine Greene wrote, "authentically present to one another," I am devastated (Greene, 1988, p.16). And so, I leave.

There have been several times over the past few years when I have been tempted to leave C&P. Organizations—whether made up of little girls intent on becoming bigger girls with the right character; congregations devoted to going to heaven and judging sin; or educators dedicated to "integrat[ing], interrogat[ing], and develop[ing] curriculum and pedagogical theories into action for educational empowerment and social justice"— are "gathering[s] of diverse individuals seeking…" *something* together. I have always presumed that the point of the Organization is to advance those (ostensibly) shared values and goals.

I am attracted to the Curriculum and Pedagogy Group (C&P) because I share its stated values and goals. I appreciate that it offers a venue for a meeting of minds—a shared space to engage in discussions related to the role that education might play in promoting the common good. In my personal and professional desire to enact this vision with ethical fidelity, it has been my hope that having such an organization in place would lead to conversations and actions that take place both in and out of the C&P auditorium—all toward promoting equitable well-being and social responsibility via education.

However, I worry that C&P, like many organizations developed around good intentions, runs the risk of becoming overly authoritative and self-indulgent. I worry that, as an organization, C&P has become too much about taking care of C&P. This mirrors issues related to our own civic government, an organization whose role ideally is to support and protect the well-being of the people who created it, and instead has become about rules, procedures, partisanship and game-playing at the direct cost of the people for whom (and by whom) it was created. When it seems that there is more energy invested in sustaining the organization than there is in the work that the organization was designed to support, then, to me, the organization has lost its value. So, while I deeply value what the *people* in C&P do in their professional lives and what I can learn from them and what I can share, I have become deeply conflicted about the local and larger structural elements of the Organization that, to me, greatly detract from the work we have begun.

If there is an assumption that we all love and value the Organization, C&P, it is mistaken. I *don't* love and value C&P. What I value are the possibilities within the work that people do to advance the common good. This raises another question about whether the work is enacted for the common good, or for the needs of still another Organization: academia, specifically the structures inherent in promotion and tenure. Henderson wonders in this book's introduction: "Does the C&P Group exist mainly as a venue for conference presentations and peer-reviewed publications, particularly for newer members of the academy?" This is a question that comes to my mind, too. After attending annual conferences (not just C&P, but *all* of them), I usually come back feeling depressed. My impressions are that the hoped-for and eagerly anticipated meeting of minds becomes instead so much about puffing chests, jockeying for position, and impressing other members of the group. The depression also comes because I cannot see how what we are saying and writing is actually having impact on the lives of the schoolchildren who I spend time with and who *need* "educational reform and social change" to happen.

In Girl Scouts, we had a mission statement that claimed a vision of nurturing courageous, confident girls with character to make "the world a better place." But, mostly what we did was attend meetings and study the steps toward acquiring badges. Our troop became focused on earning a *lot* of badges rather than on what might be helpful in building our confidence and courage to change the world. My three badges were for pet care (while wondering why we were finding dogs to bathe in order to earn a cloth badge rather than bathing dogs because they needed a bath); books (wondering why I needed a badge to prove I liked to read); and for cooking (wondering why we were baking cookies for a badge when it seemed like the best reason to bake them would be out of deep respect for the genius who thought that melting dark chocolate bits in cookie dough would be a good idea). I never got around to sewing my three badges on to my sash, and so I usually pinned or stapled mine on the morning of meeting days when we wore our uniforms to school. This was frowned on, and I remember my troop leader, Mrs. Barron, threatening to take my badges away if I did not sew them on. But she never did (just *talked* about it). It was not long before I felt a disconnect between what I hoped to experience as a member of my troop, and what was actually happening. I did not care about the badges (even though I liked taking care of animals and reading books), and I felt no allegiance to the Troop; my allegiance was to the ideas and possibilities that brought the troop together in the first place.

So, the question looms — is it time for me to exist stage left once again? And if so, where would I go to enact the vision that C&P so eloquently articulates?

In the introduction, Henderson shares Maxine Greene's comforting "I am not yet" — and as he does, I resonate with her ease with being in flux, in progress; and realize full well that I, too, am not yet. It occurs to me that I am looking to the organization, C&P to BE (not *become*) the dream of goodness and generosity that I hope to see in the world. It is unrealistic and unfair to expect the organization to BE what I hope for. Instead, perhaps we (the organization and I) can work together toward *becoming*.

I began this essay ready to share a desire to leave C&P for the same reason that I left my girl scout troop 46 years ago, bemoaning: "All we ever do at those conferences is talk about what we're *going* to do or *should be* doing." But, I have changed my mind. I must also allow for the opportunities that occur due to being a part of this group. While I will not *love* C&P, I can acknowledge about me and C&P: *We* are not yet.

Reference

Greene, M. (1988). *The dialectic of freedom*. New York: Teachers College Press.

The Moral Imperative to Essentialize: The Next Challenge for Curriculum and Pedagogy

DONNA ADAIR BREAULT
Northern Kentucky University

As scholars deeply committed to influencing practice, we face a critical and moral imperative to essentialize. In order to involve ourselves in crossing boundaries — both disciplinary and professional — we must hold back our ideology and our professional passions to the degree that we are then able to connect meaningfully with others. Sennett (2004) describes this form of holding back for the sake of community by comparing it to what happens to musicians when they are part of a string quartet. According to Sennett, each musician in a quartet must, at times, hold back within a musical piece so that other members of the quartet can be heard. Thus, in order to function as part of the quartet, the musician must see his or her identity as part of something larger than him or herself. Even though the musician is highly skilled and passionate about his or her instrument, the collective work of the quartet prevails. Likewise, as scholars we are heavily invested in and passionate about our own ideology. Nevertheless, in order to use the association as an instrument for change, we must recognize that the collective and democratic work of the association must be more important than our personal agendas.

Holding back our passions and ideological trajectories is challenging enough, but if we really want to help bring about change in schools, then we must do even more. We must embrace the practitioner vernacular in spite of the ideological challenges it may pose. We must see current "problems of practice" as necessary foci for work within our association. Most practitioners are forced to operate from very narrow yet powerful "word boxes" developed by policy makers, politicians, and educational corporations selling reform models, testing packages, and the like. Many of these word boxes focus on accountability. If we ignore this vocabulary and the corresponding problems practitioners are facing, then we cannot possibly influence practice in meaningful ways. Yes, we want practitioners to engage their educational imaginations for the sake of justice and democratic schooling, but as Dewey (1933) has warned, "The aims and ideals that move us are generated through imagination. But they are not made out of imaginary stuff. They are made out of the hard stuff of the world of physical and social experience" (p. 34). Practitioners need to be able to abstract meaningful alternative images of schooling from ideology designed to solve current problems. As Dewey (1946) further admonished, our theorizing needs not merely solve the problems of theorizers. It must, first and foremost, solve the problems of practitioners. We cannot expect teachers and administrators to independently translate highly theorized autobiographical inquiry or make connections between their own work and theorizing about culture, media, and identity.

Many times over the years practitioners have attended the conference. Many of these practitioners were doctoral students. Nevertheless, they often lamented that they did not understand much of what they heard and they found even less relevant for their work. I believe part of the ideological distance between conference presenters and practitioners is a result of a lack of ideological diversity overall within the conference. Comfortable ideological trajectories—particularly in collective form - do not generate complicated conversations because there is no tension between the participants. Brilliant theorizing springs forth. Interesting metaphors abound, and colleagues nod and agree with one another. While highly abstract, the conversations in most Curriculum and Pedagogy sessions are far from complicated because most attendees agree with the presenters. Most attendees feel comfortable with the vocabulary and the ideas of the presentations because it is so similar to their own work.

This is problematic because it contradicts basic tenets of the association. From the beginning the conference set out to bring together different voices. Two of the original five goals in the first town hall addressed this need for free exchange including diverse perspectives:

> Proposition 2: Invite, promote, and value *dissimilar* positions and perspectives among participants.

> Proposition 4: Invite, promote, and value participants representing the *broad range of curriculum work*.

On most accounts, the nature of each year's program has reflected a general leaning in terms of our theorizing, and whatever limited diversity did exist was typically a result of the work of a few more practitioner-oriented graduate students, many of whom attend for only one year. We have not actively pursued scholars whose views differ significantly from our own. When we have managed to get a professor with different views to present at the conference, we really do not provide enough spaces where he or she would feel welcomed throughout the conference. In those instances, the professor has typically come only to present and then leave. Further, the language of our calls for proposals is often slanted in such a way that individuals who are more involved with curriculum work (whether disciplinary work in universities or administrative work in school districts) do not feel comfortable submitting their work for the conference. Further, on the rare occasion we have had someone come in and challenge us, those challenges did not develop into meaningful conversations. Both in the case of Bill Wraga attending in 2003 and Deron Boyles and Phillip Kovaks presenting in 2005, attendees respectfully listened, but they failed to engage beyond the boundaries of the sessions.

We have many opportunities to "perform solo" in our professional lives. Academic journals and other professional conferences give us a great deal of space to display our ideological passions and expertise. However, if we want Curriculum and Pedagogy to be different—to make a difference—then we need to follow Sennett's challenge and hold back. We should suppress our passions, egos, and agendas in order to genuinely achieve complicated conversations that will support a dynamic professional association. Only then will we be able to approximate the grand and noble aims originally established for the Curriculum and Pedagogy Group.

References

Dewey, J. (1933). A common faith. In J. A. Boydston's (Ed.), *The Later Works of John Dewey, Vol. 9 (1933-1934)*. Edwardsville, IL: Southern Illinois University Press.
Dewey, J. (1946). *The problems of men*. New York: Greenwood Press.
Sennett, R. (2004). *Respect in a world of inequality*. New York: W. W. Norton Company.

September 1, 2010

Dear Jim,

I usually don't pay attention to astrology, as my critical, analytical self (ironically, these words describe my Virgoan astrological self) more often than not trumps ancient metaphysics. However, I found it hard to ignore a recent email from Vicki Noble, a self-described "feminist shamanic healer, author, scholar and wisdom teacher," in which she described the current astrological condition of Mercury in retrograde (August 20 through September 27, 2010) as a period

> when we are advised to recall, revisit, renew, restore, rework, rethink, review, remember, return, repair, re-enter, reconvene, and so on. Anything that requires us to go back into the past and pick up a lost stitch or bring up a forgotten moment is supported when Mercury is in its apparent backward movement (V. Noble, personal communication, August 28, 2010).

My personal life has been manifesting these activities in an uncanny way. I made a summer journey to my childhood home, and acquired of boxes of ancestral photographs and my great grandmother's fine china, silver, and crystal, all evoking forgotten moments and memories. I've experienced an inexplicable compulsion to polish, clean, dust, sort, mend, discard, and rearrange, and to restore and repair antique furniture and rugs. I've had dreams in which I ritually enact the healing and repair of old loves. Picking up threads and lost stitches in conscious and unconscious realms. So this is perhaps an opportune time to collect and revisit your past writings, with an eye to recalling, revisiting, renewing, restoring, reworking, rethinking, reviewing, remembering, returning, repairing, re-entering, re-convening (I know how much you like verbs!)

First, I must express my admiration for you, Jim, and for your seemingly inexhaustible capacity to enact "ethical fidelity" in your personal and professional lives. We have worked together on many projects over the years and I know no one who so consistently works and reworks ideas, fine tuning them, graciously accepting feedback and criticism, collaborating sincerely with others and doing their best to "walk the talk." Your service to the mission of C&P has been exemplary and you certainly embody the notion of the "lead learner." In fact, your zest for new scholarly projects and enthusiasm for the very practical work of institutionalizing democratic leadership projects leave me slightly breathless.

We both began our educational "vocations" in the 1970's, a heady era in which dusty window curtains were yanked back and doors were flung open, letting in light and air and possibility. For me, it was a decade of community organizing, protest, and consciousness-raising, of Foxfire, deschooling, unschooling and planning radical educational conferences, and of creating alternative schools, alternative communities, alternative living arrangements, alternative architecture, alternative spirituality— you name it, the operative word was "alternative." Alternative to the soul destroying, mind-numbing, ecologically ruinous, bureaucratic, capitalist, conformist, consumer culture we had been born and bred to. Unlike the more cynical, realistic youth culture of today, we were confident that we could and would change absolutely everything, in at most, 20 years, simply by living the ideals that we held. Perhaps it is Mercury in retrograde, with its energy of introspection, or perhaps it is the times themselves. But I am feeling a sort of psychic fatigue, the fatigue that comes from decades of unrelenting attacks on the educational ideals that were birthed in this earlier era and which I have tried to carry forward into my professional life.

Like you, I was drawn to the creative energy of the founding C&P group in the late 1990's, with its aim to "advance public moral leadership in education through dialogue and action...and to bring together individuals from diverse settings, including school district curriculum leaders and K-12 teachers, non-governmental community groups and organizations, graduate students and scholars from public schools to universities who seek to integrate, interrogate, and develop curriculum and pedagogical theories into action for educational empowerment and social justice." Though I deeply appreciated the exchange of ideas at the Bergamo Conference, this new organizational entity promised a higher level of connection between theory and action, and I felt that given the increasingly reactionary educational environment of standardization, testing, and the narrowing of curriculum possibilities, academics simply had to become more activist in promoting progressive ideas and supporting school people who were struggling to engage in authentic democratic "curriculum and pedagogy."

To me, the heart of your work to define the C&P mission is captured in your second editor's essay (Vol. 1, #2) when you acknowledge the importance of the 1995 text, *Understanding curriculum* with your appreciation of the ways in which that book clarified the "eclectic arts" at the heart of disciplined curriculum work, but note that it falls short of elaborating the ways in which "complicated conversations" might find expression in "deliberative artistry." Your explicit linking of curriculum and pedagogy, developed and articulated in your essays, will surely mark an historical recommitment of at least some in the curriculum field to try and make their work matter in the everyday context of schooling.

In the spirit of recalling, reviewing, and remembering our C&P mission statement, and speaking only from my own limited personal perspective, here's what I think we have accomplished. We have created another curriculum conference, differing only slightly from the other major curriculum gatherings—Bergamo, AAACS, and Professors of Curriculum—all of which I have felt privileged to be a part of. The efforts of C&P to be more democratic with its governing council and town meetings have been impressive, but I am not sure to what extent we have truly broadened our scope as widely as we had hoped in the beginning. And this is through no fault of individual members; rather, it seems related to the nature of academic organizations themselves and the professional requirements of teaching, publishing, research and tenure. We have a marvelous journal, thanks to the indefatigable efforts of you and Patrick and the many contributions from editorial assistants and scholars who made it happen regularly. But I suspect it is read primarily by our membership. I do enjoy reading the words of my colleagues and appreciating the depth and breadth of the thinking in our scholarly community, but in terms of outreach, I'm not sure an academic journal will ever get us where we want to be in terms of impacting policy. Perhaps academic conferences and journals are and should remain places for us to exchange ideas and fertilize new thinking, to renew relationships, and inspire us with the strength, stamina, and direction to pursue our local projects. To hope for more may be to place unrealistic expectations on our time and energies.

I recently met with members of a new generation of educational activists, who have conceived and initiated a progressive educational organization/network, IDEA (The Institute for Democratic Education in America), whose mission and ideals are consistent in important ways with those of the Curriculum and Pedagogy Group. I have been thoroughly impressed with this group of young people. They are organized for action, strategic, completely tapped in to the new digital social networking tools, and savvy about grassroots politics and praxis. They are not scholars, but they are intelligent, and they think in meaningful and critical ways about education policies and practices. And unlike activists of an earlier generation (remember the maxim to not trust anyone over 30?), they are committed to a multigenerational approach, and believe that culture can be transformed when three generations or more are present. Most important, they are on fire and energetic, and blessedly free of the fatigue that I have been prone to in regards to the possibilities for progressive educational change. They are also free of the requirements of research, teaching, and publishing, and hence have their time and energy liberated to engage in ACTION. I am contributing what I can to their work, in ways that make sense in terms of my time and energy.

Perhaps it is in relationships and activities like these—rhizomatic, situation-specific, strategic interventions in local nodes—that the mission of C&P can best be realized. I imagine that many of our members form such alliances for action from time to time, and that the work we do has been nurtured and advanced by the complicated conversations we have had over time. Thus, we might never fully grasp the "success" of our organization or the efficacy of our mission statement, for like ripples from multiple stones thrown into a deep pond, the effects of our actions and our "truth events" (à la Badiou) must remain, forever, unfathomable.

Sincerely Yours,

Kathleen Kesson
Long Island University, Brooklyn Campus

The Path Less Taken: Immanent Critique in Curriculum and Pedagogy

Conclusion

JAMES G. HENDERSON
Kent State University

I begin this concluding chapter with two stories that highlight the challenges of practicing **immanent critique** in two specific curriculum and pedagogy contexts. Because I will be discussing two ways that the theoretical discussion in this book's introductory chapter can be translated into practice, both narratives are context-specific illustrations of the Curriculum and Pedagogy (C&P) Group's mission "to advance public moral leadership in education through dialogue and action." These narratives will also provide further insights into why **immanent critique** is the 'path less taken' in progressive educational work. I will begin by expanding on a brief account that was composed for one my *Journal of Curriculum and Pedagogy's* Editors' Introduction essays (Volume 5, Number 1, Summer, 2008) that is reprinted in Part I of this book. I will then tell the story of the work on a pilot Teacher Leader Endorsement Program (TLEP), which will be completed in December, 2010. After telling these two stories, I will review the contents of this book and share some final reflections on why this book was written.

Introducing a Lead Learner Conception

My Part I account of the work on the state-mandated North Central Association for Teacher Education (NCATE) assessment for the Curriculum and Instruction (C&I) Master's Degree Program at Kent State University ended with the note that the C&I faculty was currently finalizing the details of their assessment approach. That design work has now been completed, and the assessment process is currently underway during the current Fall, 2010 semester. As mentioned in the Part I essay, graduate students are introduced to the assessment in an introductory C&I course entitled, "Fundamentals of Curriculum." The course begins with the study and discussion of three interrelated curriculum problem solving paradigms as described in Henderson and Gornik (2007):

- **Standardized management** with its focus on facilitating standardized test performances enforced by state accountability mandates. March and Peters' (2008) *Designing Instruction: Making Best Practices Work in Standards-Based Classrooms* serves as an exemplar of this problem solving orientation.

- **Constructivist best practice** with its focus on facilitating performances of understanding informed by one or more of the academic or vocational/technical disciplines. This category of performances is, generally, the referent for 'best practices' in professional educational associations. Wiggins and McTighe's (2005) *Understanding by Design* serves as an exemplar of this problem solving orientation.

- **Curriculum wisdom** with its focus on facilitating the problem of performances of understanding informed by one or more of the academic or vocational/technical disciplines and by discourse on democratic freedoms/responsibilities, including the mission statements of most educational organizations. Henderson and Gornik's (2007) *Transformative Curriculum Leadership* serves as an exemplar of this problem solving orientation.

Students learn that each paradigm advances a particular interpretation of educational standards and professional accountability/responsibility. They also learn that there are complicated developmental and political tensions enveloping the three problem-solving paradigms and that addressing these tensions requires arts of deliberation and negotiation. The following general rationale for this course design is carefully explained and discussed at the first class:

> All nations on the planet are currently confronting and addressing global interdependence and information age conditions—hence, the importance of teaching for understanding that is tied to one or more of the academic or vocational disciplines. Many of these nations have established a 'democratic' social contract—hence, the importance of teaching for a personal and social understanding of responsible democratic living.

As part of the course requirement, students must complete three papers. The first written assignment is a critique of a specific curriculum action. Students begin by studying key principles of good critical work in education as presented in Walter and Soltis (2009):

> We want to know what happened, why it happened, and if something can be done to improve matters. ...Criticism, both in the narrow sense of finding fault and in the wider sense of analyzing and evaluating, is an important form of curriculum theorizing carried out by curriculum specialists. Instead of proposing a curriculum and rationalizing it, the scholarly critic assesses the strong and weak points of either an existing curriculum theory or an existing program. ...Criticism normally also offers a summary assessment of what it has been critical about: All things considered, what should we make of it or do about it? (pp. 69-71)

Students then initiate their critical case study, using the following set of questions as a guide. What is the specific curriculum action? Who is involved in the activity, and what are the pragmatic consequences of this work? Describe the underlying *processes* of the curriculum action and the specific *products* that resulted from these processes. Has any thought been given to a defensible conceptualization of 'curriculum,' or are the curriculum decision-makers simply (and unconsciously) following certain habits, customs, and/or ideologies? What are the aims of the curriculum work? Are there any inconsistencies between the promised curriculum problem solving (as articulated or inferred in the organizational mission statement) and the enacted problem solving? If there are inconsistencies, are they being addressed through professional development activities? Is the curriculum action viewed as a 'reform' effort? If so, how is the "reform" interpreted? Are negotiations part of the curriculum action, and do these negotiations involve any of the three curriculum problem solving paradigms? If so, how are the negotiations handled? Do the negotiations provide any insights into power relations?

The second written assignment emerges out of this critical work. Students are asked to consider how they might function as a particular type of "lead learner" (Barth, 2008) who constructively addresses the weaknesses and limitations of the curriculum action they have just critiqued. Now that they have gained experience with the critique of a specific curriculum action, how can they invite colleagues to join them in learning more about the complex developmental and political tensions associated with an inclusive approach to all three curriculum problem solving paradigms? More specifically, how can they initiate and facilitate a formal or informal professional learning community (PLC) that focuses on the *disciplined* study and practice of curriculum wisdom in the context of standardized management accountability systems and constructivist best practice advocacies? In effect, how can they initiate and sustain a disciplined professional learning community (DPLC)? What are the "freedom from" and "freedom to" (Greene, 1988) implications of this professional development work? Will the successful enactment of the DPLC require supportive public intellectual activities, such meetings or other educational events for school board members and/or local progressive community leaders?

The third written assignment draws on the critical study and lead learner assignments. Students are asked to compose a scholarly personal narrative (SPN) in which they tell the story of their *journey of understanding* while completing the case critique and professional leadership projects. The general guidance for this personal narrative is Nash's (2004) ten tentative guidelines for writing scholarly personal narratives and Henderson and Gornik's (2007) final advice on composing transformative curriculum leadership stories. Students read this guidance and advice at the beginning of the course in preparation for this SPN work, and they are asked to keep a personal journal of their course learning experiences to assist them with the creation of their narrative.

They are asked to address the following specific questions when composing their stories:

- What is in my past that works for and/or against the process of understanding the three interrelated curriculum problem solving paradigms?

- Can I envision a professional future where I and, hopefully, other educational colleagues, would engage in the disciplined study and practice these four transactions: (1) through collaborative conversations, we will inquire into the nature and relevance of holistic educational standards; (2) through collaborative conversations, we will inquire into the experiential learning implications of these holistic standards; (3) to the degree possible, we will collaboratively engage in the arts of systemic deliberation and negotiation; and (4) we will share scholarly self-examinations of our journeys of understanding.

- Considering feedback from a 'critical friend' in this class who has read a draft of my SPN, how do I see myself 'positioned' with reference to the illustrative signposts associated with transformative curriculum leadership?[1]

- Am I currently satisfied with how I am positioned with reference to the following professional standard for the C&I Master's Degree Program:

Educators will demonstrate the necessary disciplinary understanding to practice a resourceful and democratic curriculum-based pedagogy; and they will consider the possibility of serving as 'transformative' curriculum leaders for this professional artistry.[2]

At the conclusion of the introductory "Fundamentals of Curriculum" course, students are invited to continue to develop themselves as **lead learners** as they take the remaining C&I courses in their particular specializations; and they are told that they will review and update their SPN in the C&I Master's Degree Program's capstone seminar, "Critical Reflections in C&I." As part of this invitation for continuing professional development, they complete a brief self-assessment form entitled, "A Qualitative and Quantitative Snapshot of Your SPN."[3] This evaluation instrument, which was developed and refined during the 2009-2010 academic year, asks the students to assess how they think they are positioned with reference to the transformative curriculum leadership signposts. This **lead learner** self-assessment will be collected, collated and analyzed each semester in preparation for the next NCATE site visit, which will occur during the Fall, 2015 semester.

I cannot include a discussion of the C&I Master's Degree Program's capstone seminar since the course syllabus has not yet been finalized. Most likely, there will not be a sufficient number of C&I Master's Degree students who will need to take this seminar until the Fall, 2011 semester. In the meantime, the students, who have been introduced to **immanent critique** in curriculum and pedagogy, as presented in "Fundamentals of Curriculum," will be busy taking other required and elective C&I courses, a required educational research course, and additional electives. They must complete a minimum of 32 graduate credits to receive their master's degree.

---

[1] The illustrative signposts are included in this book as Appendix B.
[2] Additional background information on the C&I Master's Degree Program Standard is presented in Appendix C in this book.
[3] The form is included in this book as Appendix D.

Addressing a Professional Development Challenge

Due to the 'path less taken' nature of **immanent critique**, there is potential problem with this program design. Though the C&I faculty at Kent State University have unanimously embraced the C&I Master's Degree Program's standard, they are not necessarily prepared to actively support their students' **lead learner** development in the graduate courses they teach. This should not be surprising given that current Ph.D. socialization generally focuses on knowledge specialization without addressing the applied wisdom implications of this scholarship (Bender, 1993).[4] This characteristic of higher education emerged in the late 19th century with the initiation of "modern" research universities, as pioneered by Johns Hopkins University and the University of Michigan. This is a complex topic that, necessarily, lies outside the scope of my narrative; however, I will briefly touch on this historical reality by posing three questions linked to the book's organizing concept:

- With reference to their organization's mission statement, how many education professors could teach **immanent critique** in curriculum and pedagogy as advanced in this book?

- In fact, how many education professors would find this question professionally irrelevant, and perhaps even impertinent, pointing out that their area of specialization within the broad C&P field is mathematics education, literacy education, social studies education, early childhood education, and so on; and not curriculum studies?

- Additionally, how many curriculum studies scholars, who have cultivated a critical specialization but have not acquired a historical, "vertical" understanding of their field (Pinar, 2007), could or would want to teach **immanent critique** in curriculum and pedagogy?

These questions foreground a potential higher education roadblock that is being addressed in Kent State's C&I Master's Degree Program during the 2010-2011 academic year. C&I faculty are being invited to participate in set of professional development activities that are drawn from an elective "Curriculum Leadership" course in the C&I Master's Degree Program. Though I have taught this graduate course a number of times over the past ten years, the seminar was completely redesigned in May, 2010 to better

---

[4] This historical circumstance is quite ironical given the fact that, in etymological terms, a Ph.D. degree is a doctorate in the love of wisdom.

support the C&I Master's Degree Program new curriculum leadership standard. I taught this new course twice during Kent State's 2010 summer semester—an on-campus version with eighteen graduate students and an off-campus version with seventeen experienced teachers at a local Akron, Ohio suburban school district.

Though the two courses were taught in slightly different ways, they were both based on the same underlying design. The syllabi for both graduate seminars were specific applications of the **immanent critique** argument that was presented in this book's introductory chapter and then further amplified in the Part I essays. With the support of four textbooks and eighteen electronic reserve selections (book chapters and published articles), students were asked to consider how they could initiate and sustain the study and practice of the four transformative curriculum leadership (TCL) transactions with colleagues and/or other curriculum stakeholders in the context of a disciplined professional learning community (DPLC) activity supported by one or more public intellectual events. They first examined and discussed the following guiding principles that underlie the four TCL transactions:

- As specific applications of Gadamer's (1975) hermeneutics, the four transactions are exercises in disciplined, open-minded, open-hearted dialogue focusing on the broadening of personal horizons. Consequently, the transactions are necessarily voluntary in nature. Care must be taken that the open, 'playful' nature of these conversations is not constrained or suppressed by conscious and/or unconscious 'power-over' machinations. Pinar, Reynolds, Slattery, and Taubman's (1995) argument for curriculum work as a multifaceted, complicated conversation informs this principle.

- The conversations do not necessarily result in consensus. Tolerating differences in opinion and agreeing to disagree are necessary features of the dialogue. Rancière's (2010) discussion of "egalitarian" dissensus informs this principle.

- The four transactions are a proactive approach to learning through experience. This principle is informed by Dewey and Bentley's (1949) argument that transactional knowing lies at the heart of educative experience.

- The four transactions are an application of Fay's (1987) "fully developed" critical theory. Individually and collectively, the four transactions balance "freedom from" and "freedom to" considerations, as discussed and illustrated in Greene (1988). Consequently, transformative curriculum leadership (Henderson & Gornik, 2007) is facilitated by "lead learners" (Barth, 2008) who undertake a particular disciplined study and invite others to join them in this disciplinary engagement. In short, they are lead 'students' of four transactions.

- The four transactions are an application of Badiou's (2001) "ethical fidelity." Individually and collectively, the four transactions are inspired by Dewey's and Greene's 'love of wisdom' projects (Henderson & Kesson, 2004), which Garrison (1997) characterizes as the enactment of "eros." Given the etymology of the 'democratic' term (i.e., power of the people), such projects are necessarily be grounded in "for all" inclusivity (Badiou, 2001).

After examining and discussing these five principles, the graduate students study the four transformative curriculum leadership transactions through a particular disciplinary lens. Pinar (2007) argues that there are disciplinary features in curriculum studies but no underlying disciplinary structure, and he uses the term "disciplinarity" to make this subtle distinction. He introduces this distinction by first acknowledging contemporary curriculum scholars' well-justified skepticism toward any form of disciplinary normalization and surveillance. Pinar (2007) then defines curriculum disciplinarity as the practice of an "intellectual labor of understanding" (p. xii) and notes that curriculum disciplinarities are "more intellectual dispositions than inviolate orderings" (p. xiii).

The four TCL transactions are presented as intellectual dispositions requiring a 'labor' of understanding through disciplined study as interpreted by Pinar (2005):

> Not instruction, not learning, but study constitutes the process of education, a view, McClintock (1971) tells us, [that is] grounded in "individuality," "autonomy," and "creativity." (p. 167) ...From the point of view of study, self-formation follows from our individual appropriation of what is around us; this capacity for selection, for focus, for judgment, McClintock (1971) suggests, is the great mystery to be solved. This is, I submit, the mystery that autobiography purports not to solve, but to portray and complicate. (p. 70)

Students' disciplined study is guided by the following four questions:

- **How do we understand education as the enactment of holistic democratic purposes, as the practice of a democratic "*Bildung*?"**
  The concept of *Bildung* refers to the interplay between character

and cultural formation as the aim of education. Westbury, Hopmann, and Riguarts (2000) write that the study of *Bildung* emerged in Prussia (now, Germany) at the end of the 18th century and that "the word *Bildung* or 'formation' as its 'embodiment,' was decisively important for the future of German thinking about teaching and schooling, and of the German professions and culture more generally" (p. 24). There is no such comparable tradition in American education; however, there is a tradition in the United States of recognizing the 'holistic' challenge of educating for both cognitive and psychosocial development. Dewey's work on linking holistic educational experiences to democratic cultural building informs this study (Dewey, 1938/1998; Jackson, 2002). The notion of teaching for '3S' understanding, which refers to the interplay of **S**ubject understanding with 'democratic' **S**elf and **S**ocial understanding, serves as scaffolding for this personal/cultural orientation (Henderson & Gornik, 2007).

- **How do we understand the facilitation of experiences that advance holistic democratic purposes?** Dewey's body of work provides, of course, key resources for the study of this question. There is a huge amount of current literature on the notion of experiential learning; however, care must be taken when examining this topic since 'educational experience' can be interpreted in many different ways. The study/conversational focus here is on holistic educational experiences—for teachers and students—which advance a democratic *Bildung* agenda. With reference to teaching for 3S understanding, how do educators come to understand all of the complexities and nuances of this pedagogical challenge? Henderson and Gornik (2007) present a multimodal scaffolding that balances inquiry into subject matter understanding (Wiggins & McTighe, 2005) with poetic, critical, multiperspective, ethical and political questioning.

- *How do we understand education as the practice of systemic deliberative artistry?* The first part of this question addresses the "ecological" nature of curriculum and pedagogy (Eisner, 1994). As Henderson and Gornik (2007) note, there is a close and vital interdependence between planning, teaching, evaluating and organizing deliberations. In the context of the dominant standardized management paradigm, walls are often built between these naturally overlapping deliberative domains so that the 'left hand' often does not know what the 'right hand' is doing. Design decisions are separated from planning and teaching decisions which, in turn, are separated from evaluation decision making; and organizational decisions are often made without teachers' deliberative input.   Structures are established, and teachers are not allowed to question them. This third area of study focuses on how to begin to break down these bureaucratic and political barriers, including the barriers between the three curriculum problem solving paradigms. Directing standardized achievement and engaging in constructivist best practices may be part of the deliberative repertoire, not as unexamined ideological scripts, but as elements in case-based decision-making. Schwab's (1978) work on deliberative artistry, particular his discussions of the practical and eclectic arts, is a key starting point for this study. There is a vast amount of literature on the topic of curriculum and teaching deliberations, and Walker (2003) provides a good overview of this literature. Again, care must be taken in this area of study to examine interpretations of "deliberation" that support education as *Bildung* and education as the facilitation of appropriate holistic experiences.

- *How do we share disciplined self-examinations of our journeys of understanding?* This study and conversation question addresses the challenge of rethinking the Latin noun, *curriculum*, which literally refers to an educational course that students run (i.e. an educational course of action) to the Latin gerund, *currere*, which literally refers to the running of the educational course (Pinar & Grumet, 1976). When curriculum is interpreted as currere, the focus is on the continuity between past, present and future learning moments. In essence, interpreting curriculum as currere highlights the 'journey' dimension of educational experience. In the context of 3S pedagogy, educators' journeys understanding are foregrounded. Henderson and Gornik (2007) make the critical point that educators will not be in the position to facilitate their students' 3S understanding if they themselves are not engaged in parallel journeys of understanding. They conclude each chapter of their book with a currere essay written by Rosemary Gornik. In their groundbreaking text on currere, Pinar and Grumet (1976) frame the past/present/future self-examination of currere in psychoanalytical terms. In an important sequel to this co-authored book, Pinar (2004) advances currere as a balanced self-examination and social critique. There is a vast amount of literature on the currere topic.

It is assumed that most, if not all, of the C&I faculty at Kent State University don't have the time to read the four texts and eighteen book chapters and articles in the "Curriculum Leadership" course. Therefore, they will be introduced to an abbreviated version of this study agenda. Hopefully, this professional development work will provide them with sufficient background to actively encourage and cultivate their students' **immanent critique** and **lead learner** capacities.

Because the standard for the C&I Master's Degree Program was unanimously passed after a year of faculty discussions and revisions, I am optimistic that this professional development work will be embraced. However, time will tell if my optimism is warranted. I conclude this first narrative by honestly admitting that the study and practice of **immanent critique** from a **lead learner** frame of reference may only be explicitly addressed in the C&I Master's Degree Program's introductory and capstone courses.

Enacting a Pilot Teacher Leader Endorsement Program

My second **immanent critique** story is, politically speaking, more dramatic with a potential educational policy upside.[5] In January, 2010 I began working with four Kent State University colleagues in the Educational Administration Program (Anita Varrati, Autumn Tooms, Christa Boske, and Catherine Hackney) and with my *Transformative Curriculum Leadership* co-author and former doctoral advisee, Rosemary Gornik, on a pilot Teacher Leader Endorsement Program (TLEP) for the state of Ohio. As I mentioned in the introductory chapter, this pilot project was supported by a $100,000 grant from the Ohio Department of Education (ODE). The collaborative grant work, which is currently in process and will not be completed until December, 2010, is a potentially significant ground-breaking reform effort since Ohio is the first state in the United States to provide formal policy support for teacher leadership. My story will highlight the **immanent critique** dynamics that were in play in this pilot project.

Seventeen experienced teachers from the suburban Cuyahoga Falls City School District volunteered to participate in the TLEP pilot, and they understood that when they completed the program they would have a state of

---

[5] I want to thank Rosemary Gornik for her feedback on a first draft of this narrative. Her thoughtful insights provided valuable prompts for my personal reflections.

Ohio "Teacher Leader" endorsement attached to their teaching license.[6] They were told by their Assistant Superintendent of Instruction that the school district's administrators were committed to supporting their professional leadership work. This positive, supportive scenario is currently unfolding without serious problems; and at the time of the publication of this book, the seventeen teachers were all engaged in specific leadership projects. I will refer to them as teacher leader "candidates" since they will not receive their state of Ohio endorsement until they have completed the pilot program in December.

Since the curricular centerpiece of this pilot program are the two "Fundamentals of Curriculum" and "Curriculum Leadership" courses described in this chapter, all of the teacher leadership projects are based on an **immanent critique** of the following statement: *"The mission of the Cuyahoga Falls City School District is to provide students with skills: to excel to his or her highest level, to contribute to our democratic society, and to successfully compete in a global economy."* The teacher leader candidates were asked to carefully examine the way their mission statement's key term, "skills," was interpreted across the standardized management, constructivist best practice and curriculum wisdom paradigms; and though some of the teachers expressed reservations about this multi-paradigmatic critical work at first, all of them eventually and enthusiastically practiced this **immanent critique.** In succinct terms, they recognized that *if* they did not extend their curriculum and teaching work beyond the state of Ohio's accountability systems, their students would not excel to their highest levels, contribute to their democratic society, nor successfully compete in a global economy. Brief excerpts from the scholarly personal narratives (SPNs) of two of the teacher leader candidates illustrate this emerging critical awareness:

Candidate #1

As I have been reading your [*Transformative Curriculum Leadership*] book and reflecting on my teaching and beliefs of what my job is, I am starting to encounter a small problem; I see myself in all three paradigms. Every part where it talks about standardized management, I fit in perfectly with it; I could be the poster child for it. Is it possible to have such a strong belief in our testing system and a strong belief in doing what I am told to do that any part of my teaching can be included in the curriculum wisdom paradigm?

---

[6] Cuyahoga Falls is a suburb of Akron, Ohio.

Candidate #2

While I believe I am developing an identity that can influence my professional peers as well as model of the habits of hope, I would like to do it without cheat sheets. Hopefully more will be uncovered as the course continues this summer. ...A significant complication to this transformation...is the political and economic obstacles that force so much time and effort to be spent on teaching the standards...memorizing the course data for the sake of passing the test rather than as a means to some greater public or democratic goal. ...My role as a teacher leader will be essential in transforming this dominant school paradigm to a curriculum best practices paradigm and eventually to the more holistic approach of curriculum wisdom.

Based on the multi-paradigm critical analysis of their school district's mission statement, all the teacher leader candidates enthusiastically engaged in the study of the curriculum and pedagogy 'disciplinarity,' as described above, **and** in the generative leadership implications of this practitioner scholarship. In effect, they collectively understood that their critical work would not be "fully developed" (Fay, 1987) if they did not function as **lead learners**. Klimek, Ritzenhein, and Sullivan's (2008) approach to generative leadership informed the candidates' lead learner planning:

Generative school leaders are intent on actualizing the generative capacity of their school for one very simple reason. They realize that both students and staff will learn, perform, and thrive better. Generative environments are rich in stimuli, offering challenges and contrasts to existing mental models that can catalyze new ideas and new avenues for action. Generative leaders push back on the commonplace mechanistic ways of organizing and doing business to make room for generative modes of inquiry and action. The dominant machinelike mental model of our day is unrelenting and impatient in rushing from symptom to analysis to fix. It leaves no time or mental space for inquiry, creativity, and reflection—modes of cognition that are integral stages in learning and essential to breaking out of the blindness.... Generative school leaders realize that we cannot shape new futures for our schools without the expansive impetus that generativity provides. (p. 48)

A brief *excerpt from the SPN of one of the* candidates typifies the growing awareness of all of the candidates in the importance of working as **lead**

learners engaged in the study of the four transformative curriculum leadership transactions:

> Each of us [in the cohort], I suspect has a different conception of just what we mean by teacher leadership. I think of teacher leadership as the act of having a positive influence on the school as well as within the classroom…. All teachers have leadership potential. Schools badly need the leadership of teachers. Teachers become active learners in an environment where they are leaders. When teachers lead, principals extend their own capacity; students live in a democratic, community of learners, and schools benefit from better decision making. This idea goes along with our teacher leadership cohort program. Each and every one of the participants had a different idea about what were happen as a result of this endorsement. I feel we have developed into a strong group of colleagues that can face any challenge. We were selected for this cohort because of our leadership skills. We are still leaders with much more knowledge and training.

All of the teacher leader candidates understood that their **lead learner** planning would require them to negotiate across all three curriculum problem solving paradigms, and a *drama that unfolded behind the scenes of the pilot program provides insight into the need for these negotiations. In general*, transformative curriculum leadership study and practice must take place in educational environments dominated by standardized accountability with, perhaps, some tolerance and support for constructivist best practices as advanced by such professional associations as the National Council of Teachers of Mathematics (NCTM), the National Council of Teachers of English (NCTE) and the National Council for the Social Studies (NCSS). In effect, transformative curriculum leaders must learn to work adeptly across all three paradigms, and this lesson was brought home to me in a very personal way beginning in January, 2010. I want to share this experience because it further clarifies why I think **immanent critique** is the path less taken in education.

As I have just noted, the Ohio Department of Education (ODE) gave Kent State University a grant to support the TLEP pilot, and we were one of four TLEP pilot programs in the state. Two other universities and one college also received $100,000 grants. ODE required all four pilot programs to submit a lengthy proposal tied to Ohio's new Teacher Leader Standards as part of the grant approval process. We submitted our original grant proposal to ODE in November, 2009 with a starting date of January

19, 2010. We were notified in mid-December that ODE had some questions about our pilot. There was concern that our transformative curriculum leadership emphasis was tangential to Ohio's Teacher Leader Standards. However, at that point in time, the ODE administrator in charge of the four pilot programs did not view this as a major problem; so we did receive the grant. We began our pilot work in January with the understanding that we would have to resubmit our grant proposal with a more careful explanation on how exactly we were compliant with Ohio's new teacher leader standards by April 1, 2010.

Though we would not lose our grant money if we were judged as being non-compliant with the teacher leader standards, our pilot would not be approved as an official Ohio TLEP; and this would have serious consequences for the seventeen Cuyahoga Falls candidates since they would complete our pilot program but not receive the state's new teacher leader endorsement. Given these high stakes, Rosemary Gornik and I painstakingly rewrote our grant proposal, carefully linking our lead learner definition to Ohio's teacher leader standards. Our final product, which evolved into a detailed fifty-three page report with a number of appendices, was resubmitted to ODE on March 30, 2010. We were told that our reworked report would undergo ODE peer review and that we would be given the results of this evaluation sometime in April. However, I wondered if we would actually receive evaluative feedback due to the adult developmental and political obstacles associated with our **lead learner** definition (Henderson & Kesson, 2004). With reference to the three problem solving paradigms, educators who embrace a curriculum wisdom orientation must necessarily work with, and build upon, the other two paradigms; constructivist best practice educators can work with the standardized management paradigm but do not yet understand curriculum wisdom; and standardized management educators do not yet comprehend constructivist best practice or curriculum wisdom. As it turned out, my intuition that we would not receive formal peer review feedback on our pilot program was right on target; and I will have more to say about this in a moment.

I had my first face-to-face session with the ODE administrator in charge of the four TLEP pilots in mid-March, and this gave me the opportunity to personally explain our pilot's **lead learner** approach. As I began my explanation, it was immediately obvious from her body language that she had some serious concerns. However, because she chose to remain silent, I was never able to learn the details of her concerns. I did know from past experience that educators who are embedded in the standardized management paradigm generally feel challenged by a multi-paradigmatic approach and can respond in a broad range of ways from curiosity to passivity to downright hostility; consequently, I figured that I was now caught up in a paradigm-conflict incident.

Prior to my face-to-face session with the ODE administrator, I had posed several inquiries at a general meeting for all four of Ohio's teacher leadership pilot programs; and though I had attempted to be diplomatic and tactful with my questions, there's a very good possibility that I came across as a non-complaint, uncooperative naysayer who was challenging the very basis of Ohio's teacher leadership pilot programs. Again, because I was aware that this is a potential problem with cross-paradigm communications and that the curriculum wisdom orientation is the 'path less taken' and is, therefore, a minority position, I knew that educators who are attempting to invite immanent critique must make sensitive judgments on when and how to speak and when to remain silent. However, because I also feel very passionate about a critically-informed, multi-paradigmatic approach to curriculum and pedagogy, I know that I can come off as overly zealous. I try to be careful about this; but in this instance, I may not have been successful. Consequently, my communication at the general meeting and in my personal session with the ODE administrator may not have been as artful as the situation demanded.

It is also important that I acknowledge that this administrator may have been under enormous pressures to successfully launch the teacher leader pilot programs, and the stakes may have been simply too high to seriously entertain an avant-garde, multi-paradigmatic interpretation of teacher leadership. I also need to acknowledge that all of my personal reflections are written from the **immanent critique** frame of reference advanced in this book. They are my perspectives, not those of the ODE administrator. Though I felt that I was talking to an educational administrator who was embedded in the standardized management paradigm, she may have had a very different view of the situation. However, since she decided not to share her perceptions with me, I don't know what she was thinking or how she felt. Our communications remained shrouded in a wall of silence. I began this book with a brief discussion of the importance of disciplined, open-minded and open-hearted conversations as the starting point for **immanent critique**. Since I never entered into the practice of this "art" of understanding with the ODE administrator, the possibility for a broadening of personal "horizons" was off the table (Gadamer, 1975).

There is one final reflection I want to share concerning my inability to explain this book's **lead learner** conception to the ODE administrator. Because cross-paradigm tensions were, most likely, in play, this state administrator may have felt that her basic beliefs and images about 'good' education were under attack. This is a serious matter in C&P work since, as Walker

(1971) documents, curriculum work is grounded in fundamental beliefs and images. Walker and Soltis (2009) explain:

> In studying how curriculum development groups actually worked, Walker [1971] found that they did not follow Tyler's [1949] four steps. In fact, many curriculum groups never stated objectives at all; and those that did generally did so near the end of their work, as a way of expressing their purpose to teachers, rather than at the beginning, as the fundamental starting point of their work. Their starting point appeared to be a set of beliefs and images they shared—beliefs about the content, about the students, their needs, and how they learn; about schools, classrooms, and teaching; about the society and its needs; and images of good teaching, of good examples of content and method, and of good procedures to follow. They spent a great deal of time stating and refining these beliefs, which comprised what Walter [1971] called their "platform." (p. 62)

As I attempted to communicate with the ODE administrator, she may have felt that I was challenging, and perhaps even denouncing, her C&P "platform." The possibility that such challenges of deep-seated beliefs and images can occur during cross-paradigm communications provides insight into why **immanent critique** is so fraught with difficulties. In short, it's not easy to work at the generative phase of the **lead learner** conception advanced in this book.

Returning to Klimek, Ritzenhein, and Sullivan's (2008) point that generative leaders facilitate "environments [that] are rich in stimuli, offering challenges and contrasts to existing mental models that can catalyze new ideas and new avenues for action" (p. 48), **lead learners** must be resourceful deliberators and negotiators as they introduce and attempt to inspire and sustain a new 'mental model' of *teachers working as disciplined students of four curriculum and pedagogy transactions*. In Schwab's (1978) terms, they must engage in the arts of the practical while advancing an eclectic, multiparadigmatic approach to C&P problem solving.

In a further attempt at bridge building, I initiated a follow-up phone conference with the ODE administrator a few days after our personal session. That phone call turned out to be a disaster; and in fact, it was the most hostile professional encounter that I have experienced in my forty-two years as an educator. Since I am deeply committed to practicing a 'love' of democratic wisdom, I immediately thought about Socrates and the 'reward' he received from his love of wisdom: banishment or death. I felt fortunate that I was protected by the American tradition of academic freedom. While Socrates' fate was to undergo a painful death by hemlock, my fate was to be tenured and promoted by Kent State University. Quite a contrast! I was

left wondering what my fate would be if my scholarly efforts were not protected by academic freedom. What if I worked in a police state? What
would be the personal consequences of my **lead learner** reform efforts? I
also wryly noted that the work of curriculum and pedagogy was not for the
faint of heart. Academics, who take on C&P challenges, are entering the
rough and tumble world of educational politics. They have left the ivory
tower for the 'front lines' of educational reform endeavors.

Fortunately, my story has a happy ending. Though I was not able to negotiate with the ODE administrator in charge of the state's pilot TLEPs, I
was fortunate that the Ohio Board of Regents (OBR) had responsibility for
the state's official TLEPs. Thomas Bordenkricher, who is the Associate
Vice Chancellor for Academic Quality & Assurance, is the administrator
who is in charge of Ohio's TLEPs. I called Dr. Bordenkircher immediately
after my phone encounter with the ODE administrator and asked if we
could schedule a personal talk as soon as possible. He agreed, and our
meeting took place two days later in his office in Columbus, Ohio. Our
one-hour session was extremely positive for three important reasons. First
of all, he let me know at the beginning of the meeting that OBR had a tradition of respecting educational scholarship, and he did not want to get into
the business of micro-managing research-based projects. Secondly, he was
very intrigued by Kent State's **lead learner** approach, particularly since he
had received a C&I Master's Degree from the University of Pittsburg. He
immediately understood that the questions guiding the four transformative
curriculum leadership (TCL) transactions were constructive alternatives to
the four questions guiding Tyler's (1949) dominant curriculum "rationale"
(Henderson, in press).[7] Finally, he quickly understood that educators who
were students of these four transactions would be better positioned to facilitate their students' 21st century learning, which was the formal policy rationale for Ohio's new Teacher Leader Endorsement Program.

My one-hour meeting with Associate Vice Chancellor Bordenkircher
ended with two favorable outcomes. OBR was finalizing its application
process for the official TLEPs, and all higher education institutions in Ohio
would be invited to apply. Dr. Bordenkircher asked me to serve as one of
OBR's peer reviewers, and I agreed. Prior to our meeting, Dr. Bordenkircher had read the reworked grant proposal report that Rosemary Gornik

---

[7] For well-documented historical analyses of why Tyler's (1949) rationale is still
the dominant paradigm in curriculum work, see Tanner and Tanner (2007) and
Null (2008). I will further discuss the contrast between the Tyler rationale and
TCL questioning near the end of this narrative.

and I had submitted to ODE, and he was pleased with the thoroughness of our work. Though OBR's official TLEP proposal requirements are slightly different from ODE's TLEP pilot program requirements, he accepted our reworked proposal without any further changes. He felt it would be a waste of our time to compose yet another TLEP proposal. This latter decision was finalized in a follow-up phone conference, which was led by Dr. Bordenkircher with the participation of Daniel Mahony, who is the Dean of Kent State University's College of Education, Health and Human Services (EHHS), Nancy Barbour, who is the EHHS Associate Dean for Administrative Affairs and Graduate Education, and Joanne Arhar, who is the EHHS Associate Dean for Student Services, Undergraduate Education, and Director of Teacher Education. With reference to our pilot TLEP's **immanent critique** and **lead learner** conceptions, this phone conference had two significant features. During the conversation, Associate Vice Chancellor Bordenkircher reiterated OBR's commitment to respect the work of educational scholars, and Dean Mahony made the point of expressing his respect for the curriculum studies scholarship underpinning our pilot TLEP.

These two administrative affirmations are critical components of my narrative for an important reason. Our pilot's **lead learner** approach is based on teachers functioning as *students* of four C&P transactions who, in turn, invite their colleagues and other curriculum stakeholders to engage in their own study. Without administrative respect and support for this disciplined scholarship, it will be very difficult for teachers to work as **lead learners**. They may still be able to advance their study-and-practice agenda in small informal ways, but their efforts will be institutionally circumscribed and may, consequently, have little impact on the organizational culture.

I hope my story does not paint an overly bleak, dismal picture about the possibilities for **immanent critique** in curriculum and pedagogy. In general, **lead learners** should be able to discover some "wiggle room" (Cuban, 2003, p. 35) for their transformative work. I found the necessary leverage when I initiated a meeting with Associate Vice Chancellor Bordenkircher. **Lead learners** must be constantly alert for invitational opportunities while recognizing that while the study of the four C&P transactions can be expansive and imaginative, the resulting practice might be quite limited. **Lead learners** must be patient opportunists, recognizing that their professional visions are, in most instances, enacted through 'baby steps.'

There are a few final pieces to my narrative that are also important to share. I am writing this story in September, 2010. At this point, we have been notified that we have successfully passed OBR's peer review process and that the final state approval of our TLEP should be forthcoming.[8] However, we have not yet received final word, so my narrative ends on an 'in process' note. In late June, Rosemary Gornik and I were invited to present our pilot TLEP at a statewide "Conference on Teacher Quality" that was sponsored by OBR. Our presentation was well-received, and we had an opportunity to invite Ohio's State Superintendent of Public Instruction, Deborah Delisle, who is in charge of ODE, to visit the Cuyahoga Falls City School District to observe the 2010-2011 **lead learner** projects. She was told that these projects would be initiated at the beginning of the school year. Superintendent Delisle has expressed some interest in meeting these 'pilot' teacher leaders; and if she takes this step, she will have an opportunity to see first-hand what teacher leaders in Ohio are capable of accomplishing. If this state superintendent field visit does occur, my encounters with the ODE administrator in charge of the teacher leader pilot programs could possibly end on a more positive note. Despite my negative experience with one ODE administrator, I will continue to look for opportunities to reach out to other ODE officials. I am confident that there are ODE administrators who will see the value of the **lead learner** conception we are pioneering.

We have not yet been contacted by Superintendent Delisle's office, and I leave it to the readers of this book to speculate on whether or not the State Superintendent of Public Instruction in Ohio will follow through with this visit. I have also invited Associate Vice Chancellor Thomas Bordenkricher to meet with the Cuyahoga Falls teachers. Since his office is in Columbus and he is quite busy, he does not have time to drive 100 miles to Akron. However, Dr. Bordenkricher does recognize the value of this visit, as both a learning opportunity for his office and as a symbolic statement; so he is sending one of his key administrative assistants, Corey Posey.

I will conclude this narrative with a set of explicit policy questions linked to Superintendent Delisle's possible visit and Mr. Posey's definite visit. If I have the opportunity, I will invite Superintendent Delisle and Mr. Posey to respond to these questions after they have observed the teacher leader projects in the Cuyahoga Falls City School District. In fact, I would like all educational policy leaders in Ohio to think deeply about these questions. What are the possibilities for official ODE and/or OBR support for

---

[8] We have still not received peer review feedback from the ODE administrator in charge of the pilot; and at this point, it is highly unlikely that such feedback will ever be provided. Though this matter is now moot, this continuing silence provides food for thought on the challenges of cross-paradigm communication.

immanent critique? With reference to curriculum and pedagogical work in Ohio's public schools, are ODE and/or OBR officials worried about the discrepancy between C&P mission rhetoric and problem solving reality? Are these educational officials concerned that public school districts throughout the state are promising democratic education in the context of 21st century learning but may not be delivering on their promises in their daily decision making? Will ODE and/or OBR officially support experienced teachers who are willing to address this rhetoric/reality inconsistency as **lead learners**? What would be the consequences for public education in Ohio if ODE and/or OBR did encourage and nurture such teacher leadership? Would Ohio become a lead state for 21st century democratic education in the United States? Would Ohio become the first state to formally support teacher leaders who have a deep vocation calling to actualize John Dewey's 1897 vision for progressive education, as cited in this book's introductory chapter: "The art of thus giving shape to human powers and adapting them to social service is the supreme art; one calling into its service the best of artists; that no insight, sympathy, tact, executive power, is too great for such service" (Dewey 1897/2009, p. 40)? I ended the introductory chapter with this quote, and I want to conclude my second narrative with the same quote. How many educators want to become "the best of artists" in our society?

Reviewing the Book and Pondering Its Future Relevance

This book has been designed to introduce and advance the notion of **immanent critique** in curriculum and pedagogy. As I mentioned in the introductory chapter, I came to conclusion over ten years ago that theorizing and practicing **immanent critique** would be a vitally important undertaking for the C&P Group, and the Part I essays are an articulation of that determination. I still feel that way, not only for one particular professional association, but for *all* educators who engage in the work of curriculum and pedagogy. If American educators who have a deep feel for the ideals of their profession, are not engaged in some sort of disciplined effort to 'walk their talk,' 'speak through their deeds' and 'practice what they preach,' I worry about the future health of my society and, by extension, for the future health of the planet as a whole. If those educators who experience a deep vocational calling are not able to learn ways to embody their inspirations, what are the consequences? Do these idealistic individuals quit teaching, giving up on their professional dreams; or do they quietly go about their work leaving the so-called educational leadership to managers and trainers who lack imagination, vision, and any sense of educational artistry?

This book has also been designed to illustrate a particular **lead learner** approach to **immanent critique**. The starting point for this approach is the practice of the art of understanding, as insightfully discussed by Gadamer (1975), and the practice of mature critical work, as thoughtfully outlined by Fay (1987). Educators first become students of four C&P transactions, which enables them to engage in a dynamic learning through experience tied to the "for all" (Badiou, 2001) democracy-in-education ideals of John Dewey and Maxine Greene. These 'lead' educators then seek ways to inspire, invite and encourage other educators to join them in this disciplined study.

In effect, this **lead learner** approach provides a constructive alternative to Tyler's (1949) dominant "paradigm" for curriculum development in the C&I field (Kliebard, 1992; Null, 2008; Tanner & Tanner, 2007). This can be clearly demonstrated by comparing the four questions in Tyler's (1949) rationale…

> ➤ What educational purposes should the school seek to attain?

> ➤ How can learning experiences be selected which are likely to be useful in attaining these objectives?

> ➤ How can learning experiences be organized for effective instruction?

> ➤ How can the effectiveness of learning experiences be evaluated?

…with the four questions that the teacher leader candidates in the Cuyahoga Falls City School District addressed in the context of the pilot TLEP:

> ➤ How do we understand the pursuit of holistic democratic purposes in education?

> ➤ How do we understand the facilitation of experiences that advance these purposes?

> ➤ How do we understand the practice of systemic deliberative artistry?

> ➤ How do we share disciplined self-examinations of our journeys of understanding?

Notice the contrast between Tyler's impersonal "school"—what Pinar, Reynolds, Slattery and Taubman (1995) call curriculum as "institutional text"—and the personal, collegial "we." Notice the shift from reductionist, technical precision to performances of human understanding—a shift informed by Eisner's (1994) distinction between behavioral objectives and expressive outcomes. Notice the shift from morally neutral language to "democracy as the moral standard for personal conduct" (Dewey, 1939/1989, p. 101). Notice the compartmentalization of educational goals, experiences, organization and evaluation in Tyler's rationale and the more "ecological" (Eisner, 1994), systemic deliberation in the TLEP alternative. Finally, notice the absence of self-examination in Tyler's rationale and its centrality in the TLEP alternative. Both Tyler's rationale and the TLEP alternative inquiries allow for interpretive diversity; however, only the TLEP questioning foregrounds the challenges of **immanent critique**. It's too easy to work as unimaginative managers and trainers, lacking any sense of ethical fidelity, when guided by the Tyler rationale or any current manifestation of this C&P 'engineering' logic.

The rationale for the TLEP alternative is presented in the introductory chapter and informed by the reprinted *JCP* essays in Part I. In effect, this book provides a great deal of space to explain, defend and illustrate a particular approach to **immanent critique** in curriculum and pedagogy. There are certainly others ways that this critical work can occur. A discussion of these possibilities lies outside the scope of this text; however, these alternatives are suggested in the Part II "Perspectives" section. The beauty of democratic 'town hall' conversations, as insightfully examined by Louise Allen, is the democratic airing of diverse viewpoints; and this diversity of perspectives is clearly on display in the simulated Part II 'dialogue.' As I first read through the interesting and provocative mix of theoretical concepts, personal insights, critical questions, creative ideas, autobiographical statements, pedagogical illustrations, self-examinations, poetic expressions and professional visions that constitute the simulated town meeting, I imagined these written offerings as oral, face-to-face presentations. I imagined sitting in the same room with Michael O'Malley, Israel Aguilar, Audrey Dentith, Fredrika Harper, Francis Broadway, Nancy Brooks, Andrew Gilbert, Thomas Kelly, Kathleen Kesson, Donna Adair Breault, Kent den Heyer, Sheri Leafgren, and Kris Sloan and pondering their points of view. That is why I like Jennifer Schneider's imaginative way of introducing the Part II section of this book.

The book was not designed to present a careful and thorough response to the eleven perspectives presented in Part II. However, I do feel strongly that anyone who reads through these contributions will gain further insight into the meaning of **immanent critique** in curriculum and pedagogy. In Gadamer's language, their 'horizons' will be broadened. If the Part II simulation was an actual face-to-face town meeting, I would want to probe further into the eleven personal statements and expressions from the perspective of "fully developed" critical theorizing (Fay, 1987). Accordingly, I would pursue the following four questions. How exactly would these diverse viewpoints be translated into the day-to-day work of curriculum and pedagogy, and what would be the inspirational referents for the C&P applications? Would it be Dewey's and/or Greene's body of work? If not, which 'for all' projects would ground and inform the C&P efforts?

This book has been designed to present the value of **immanent critique** in curriculum and pedagogy. Without such a critical approach, much is lost in the education profession and, consequently, in the way a society pursues its good life. If we humans do not work on living up to our ideals, particularly in the way we educate ourselves, what is the future prognosis for our societies and for our planet? How can we humans thrive, let alone survive, on a steady diet of superficial rhetoric, ideological posturing, tribal gamesmanship, and narrow problem solving? The blame games on the planet must recede into history. Honest, open, democratic soul-searching and self-examination must take their place. That is the future we educators should strive to embody in the present. That is the future we should strive to enact in our daily C&P work.

References

Badiou, A. (2001). *Ethics: An essay on the understanding of evil* (P. Hallward, Trans.). London: Verso.

Barth, R. S. (2008). Foreword. In G. A. Donaldson, *How leaders learn: Cultivating capacities for school improvement* (pp. ix-xi). New York: Teachers College Press.

Bender, T. (1993). *Intellect and public life: Essays on the social history of academic intellectuals in the United States*. Baltomore: The Johns Hopkins University Press.

Cuban, L. (2003). *Why is it so hard to get good schools?* New York: Teachers College Press.

Dewey, J. (1989). *Freedom and culture*. Buffalo, NY: Prometheus. (Original work published 1939)

Dewey, J. (1998). *Experience and education*. West Lafayette, IN: Kappa Delta Pi. (Original work published 1938)

Dewey, J., & Bentley, A. F. (1949). *Knowing and the known*. Boston: The Beacon Press.

Eisner, E. W. (1994). *The educational imagination: On the design and evaluation of school programs* (3rd ed.). New York: Macmillan.

Fay, B. (1987). *Critical social science: Liberation and its limits*. Ithaca, NY: Cornell University Press.

Gadamer, H. G. (1975). *Truth and method* (G. Barden & J. Cumming, Eds. & Trans.). New York: Seabury.

Garrison, J. (1997). *Dewey and eros: Wisdom and desire in the art of teaching.* New York: Teachers College Press.

Greene, M. (1988). *The dialectic of freedom.* New York: Teachers College Press.

Henderson, J. G. (In press). Learning through a disciplined curriculum study approach: Implications for educational leadership. *Scholar-Practitioner Quarterly.*

Henderson, J. G., & Gornik, R. (2007). *Transformative curriculum leadership* (3rd ed.). Upper Saddle River, NJ: Merrill/Prentice Hall.

Henderson, J. G., & Kesson, K. R. (2004). *Curriculum wisdom: Educational decisions in democratic societies.* Upper Saddle River, NJ: Merrill/Prentice Hall.

Jackson, P. W. (2002). *John Dewey and the philosopher's task.* New York: Teachers College Press.

Kliebard, H. K. (1992). *Forging the American curriculum: Essays in curriculum history and theory.* New York: Routledge.

Klimek, K. J., Ritzenhein, E., & Sullivan, K. D. (2008). *Generative leadership: Shaping new futures for today's schools.* Corwin Press.

March, J. K., & Peters, K. H. (2008). *Designing instruction: Making best practices work in standards-based classrooms.* Thousand Oaks, CA: Corwin Press.

McClintock, R. (1971). Toward a place for study in a world of instruction. *Teachers College Record, 73*(2), 161-205.

Nash, R. J. (2004). *Liberating scholarly writing: The power of personal narrative.* New York: Teachers College Press.

Null, J. W. (2008). Curriculum development in historical perspective. In F. M. Connelly (Ed.), *The sage handbook of curriculum & instruction* (pp. 478-490). Los Angeles: Sage Publications.

Pinar, W. F. (2004). *What is curriculum theory?* Mahwah, NJ: Lawrence Erlbaum Associates.

Pinar, W. F. (2005). The problem with curriculum and pedagogy. *Journal of Curriculum and Pedagogy, 2*(1), 67-82.

Pinar, W. F. (2007). *Intellectual advancement through disciplinarity: Verticality and horizontality in curriculum studies.* Rotterdam: Sense Publishers.

Pinar, W. F., Reynolds, W. M., Slattery, P., & Taubman, P. M. (1995). *Understanding curriculum: An introduction to the study of historical and contemporary curriculum discourses.* New York: Peter Lang.

Pinar, W., & Grumet, M. (1976). *Toward a poor curriculum.* Dubuque, IA: Kendall/Hunt.

Rancière, J. (2010). *Dissensus: On politics and aesthetics* (S. Corcoran, Ed. & Trans.). London: Continuum.

Schwab, J. J. (1978). *Science, curriculum, and liberal education: Selected essays* (I. Westbury & N. J. Wilkof, Eds.). Chicago: University of Chicago Press.

Tanner, D., & Tanner, L. (2007). *Curriculum development: Theory into practice* (4th ed.). Upper Saddle River, NJ: Merrill/Prentice Hall.

Tyler, R. W. (1949). *Basic principles of curriculum and instruction.* Chicago: University of Chicago Press.

Walker, D. F., & Soltis, J. F. (2009). *Curriculum and aims* (5th ed.). New York: Teachers College Press.

Walker, D. F. (1971). The process of curriculum development: A naturalistic model. *School Review, 80*, 51-65.

Walker, D. F. (2003). *Fundamentals of curriculum: Passion and professionalism* (2nd ed.). Mahwah, NJ: Lawrence Erlbaum Associates.

Westbury, I., Hopmann, S., & Riquarts, K. (Eds.). (2000). *Teaching as a reflective practice: The German didaktik tradition.* Mahwah, NJ: Lawrence Erlbaum Associates.

Wiggins, G., & McTighe, J. (2005). *Understanding by design* (2nd ed.). Alexandria, VA: Association for Supervision and Curriculum Development.

Contributors' Biographical Statements

Israel Aguilar is earning a Ph.D. in School Improvement at Texas State University – San Marcos and has five years of experience as a K-12 educator at the secondary and middle school levels. His research involves principal preparation and educational leadership for social justice. He has participated in an international research team studying the effectiveness of principal preparation programs, a project studying the effects of national student protest for educational equity in Chile, and has theorized possibilities for transforming principal preparation to enhance social justice leadership in schools and communities.

Louise Anderson Allen is an Associate Professor of Educational Leadership at South Carolina State University where she teaches curriculum change and design courses to school administrators. Her scholarship is focused on curriculum leadership practices and on Southern female educational leaders of the Progressive era. Her work appears in the *Journal of Curriculum and Pedagogy* and the *SAGE handbook of curriculum studies*. She is one of the founders of the C&P Conference; and served as its first treasurer, chair of the Publication Committee, and chair of the governing Council.

Donna Adair Breault, PhD, is Associate Professor of Educational Leadership at the Department of Counseling, Social Work, and Leadership, Northern Kentucky University. Her interests involve Dewey's theory of inquiry and its implications for leadership, curriculum, and images of public space. Her publications include *Urban education: A handbook for educators and parents* (co-authored with Louise Anderson Allen, 2008, Greenwood Press) as well as articles in *Educational Theory*, *The Educational Forum*, and *Educational Studies*.

Francis S. Broadway is a full professor of science education in the Department of Curricular and Instructional Studies, College of Education, The University of Akron. His teaching focus is content in the Early Childhood Classroom content methods and curriculum studies. His research agenda includes (science) curriculum and pedagogy through children's picture books, queer theory, and currere; however, much of his research is driven by inquiries of his students and his personal examination of and practical problem solving concerning himself as one who cares.

Nancy J. Brooks is an Assistant Professor at Ball State University where she teaches and studies the possibilities for philosophical hermeneutics as curriculum theory, the history of educational thought, and emerging curriculum trends. She has been a member of C&P since its inception and has previously served on the Governing Council and in a variety of leadership capacities.

Audrey Dentith is associate professor of Curriculum and Interdisciplinary Studies at the University of Texas San Antonio. She teaches courses in curriculum theories, interdisciplinary studies and research methods. Her most recent publications have appeared in Canadian Journal of Education, Sociology and Journal of Curriculum & Pedagogy. Her current interests include leadership of curriculum development in undergraduate and graduate programs in interdisciplinary studies and globalization and a community project with cross-disciplinary faculty around Latin American/Mestizo history, art, literature and culture at the San Antonio Art Museum.

Andrew Gilbert, PhD, began his career in Education as a middle and high school science teacher in the Washington, DC metro area. He is currently a member of the Master in Teaching faculty at The Evergreen State College in Olympia, WA. His research and teaching interests include connecting critical constructivist learning theories with innovative teaching practice, social justice, and the interrogation of socio-cultural factors that create and sustain inequitable structures within schools and society.

Fredrike Harper serves as the Director of Curriculum and Instruction for the Cedarburg School District near Milwaukee, Wisconsin. She has also served as a classroom teacher, curriculum specialist, and building principal. Fredrika completed her doctorate in Urban Education with an emphasis in Educational Administration at the University of WI - Milwaukee in 1996. Her scholarly focus is on progressive curriculum planning and implementation in K-12 schools.

James Henderson is a Professor of Curriculum Studies at Kent State University, where he has taught graduate courses for twenty years. His research focuses on the arts of democratic curriculum leadership, and he has individually or collaboratively published five books and over sixty essays on this topic. He helped launch the *Journal of Curriculum and Pedagogy* and served as its co-editor for first six years. He has been an officer for the

American Association for the Advancement of Curriculum Studies (AAACS) and the factotum for the Professors of Curriculum Society.

Kent den Heyer is an Associate Professor in the Department of Secondary Education, University of Alberta. Kent has a doctorate in Curriculum Studies from the University of British Columbia and Masters in the same from OISE/University of Toronto. He publishes research in curriculum studies, social studies and history education, historical consciousness, and educational philosophy. He is a past Chair of the Governing Council of the C & P group and first attended the conference in 2001.

Thomas E. Kelly is an Associate Professor of Education and Coordinator of the Adolescent and Young Adult Licensure Programs at John Carroll University. His writings and scholarly interests are in the areas of critical democratic pedagogy, curriculum studies, and addressing issues of conflict and controversy in education.

Kathleen Kesson is Professor of Teaching and Learning at the Brooklyn Campus of Long Island University, where she teaches courses in the foundations of education and teacher research. She has authored book chapters, book reviews, and academic articles and is co-author, with James Henderson, of *Curriculum wisdom: Educational decisions in democratic societies* (2004) and *Understanding democratic curriculum leadership* (1999), and editor, with Wayne Ross, of *Defending public schools: Teaching for a democratic society* (2004). Her interests include: democracy and education, critical pedagogy, aesthetics and education, and teacher inquiry and reflection.

Sheri Leafgren, formerly a primary grade educator, is an Assistant Professor in the Department of Teacher Education at Miami University. She is interested in the spiritual and moral wisdom of young children and how they find space to enact their moral and spiritual selves while wrapped securely in the swaddling clothes of the rules, procedures, and surveillance of the schoolroom. Her book, *Reuben's fall: A rhizomatic analysis of disobedience in kindergarten* (Left Coast Press, 2009), details kindergartners' moral and spirited actions in their classrooms, and offers insights into child-school relationships.

Michael O'Malley is an Assistant Professor of Educational and Community Leadership at Texas State University – San Marcos. His research interests include leadership for educational equity, public pedagogy, curriculum theory, and internationalization and education. His recent research projects have involved student protest for educational equity in

Chile, state oversight of the East St. Louis, IL urban school district, and rethinking qualitative methodologies for critical participatory research with youth. Selected publications appear in the *Journal of Curriculum Studies*, the *Journal of Curriculum and Pedagogy*, *Educational Studies*, *Sociology*, *Teaching Education*, and *Urban Education*.

Mark Ortwein is a doctoral student in the department of Teaching, Learning, and Culture at Texas A&M University. A former high school English teacher, he presently co-teaches an undergraduate theory-based course on contemporary schooling issues. His research interests include virtue epistemology, Neo-Aristotelian concepts of intellectual virtue, and the intersections between ethics and epistemology. His most recent publication appears in the *Journal of Virtue Worlds Research* (Vol. 2, No. 5) Mark is currently writing his dissertation and expects to graduate in the Summer of 2011.

Jennifer Schneider is currently working on her second year of doctorial study in Curriculum and Instruction in the school of Teaching, Learning, and Curriculum Studies at Kent State University. She has undergraduate degrees in Art Education and Art History, a master's in English Education, and teaching as well as tutoring experience, both domestically and internationally, in the Visual Arts and English. Her areas of interest include: multiple literacies, arts-based ways of knowing, and composition studies.

Patrick Slattery is Professor in the College of Education and Human Development at Texas A&M University. The central theme of his work is the promotion of a just, compassionate, and ecologically sustainable global culture through holistic and reconceptualized approaches to curriculum, constructive postmodern understandings of education, queer studies in gender and sexuality, and Process philosophical visions of creativity and change. In his research he contends that spiritual, ethical, and social transformation is intimately linked to visual culture, public pedagogy, and aesthetics and that wisdom can emerge in the artistic process.

Kris Sloan is an Associate Professor in the School of Education at St. Edward's University. He teachers course on culture, curriculum, and educational policy at the graduate and undergraduate levels. He focuses on content related to anti-oppressive education, White racism, heterosexism, and masculinity studies. He has authored numerous journal articles and book chapters on the ways curriculum policies influence the classroom practices of teachers and learning experiences of children, in particular children of color. His most recent book is, *Holding schools accountable: A handbook for educators and parents*.

Appendix A

The Journal of Curriculum and Pedagogy's Mission Statement

The *Journal of Curriculum and Pedagogy* is positioned at the intersection of curriculum theory and teaching studies. We believe that notions of professional artistry in all teaching fields are deeply embedded in general curriculum concerns and issues. We, therefore, are committed to advancing scholarship that explores the relationship between curriculum and pedagogy. The editors invite papers and other scholarly products that address curriculum and pedagogy through a wide range of interdisciplinary, transdisciplinary, or other unique multi-discursive and artistic efforts. The journal seeks to extend critical discussion and to advance research that situates education in socio-political and cultural contexts. We welcome papers and other products with a historical, philosophical, gendered, sexual, racial, ethnic, linguistic, autobiographical, aesthetic, institutional, theological, and/or international emphasis. In welcoming these many and varied modes of curriculum analyses, the editors acknowledge that there are a multiplicity of stories to be told and texts to be acknowledged in curriculum and pedagogy.

Scholarship, like teaching, involves making choices—both theoretical and practical. We recognize that the moral consequences of each educational decision impacts all aspects of curriculum and teaching work, and we acknowledge that anyone educational perspective, story, mode of instruction, or critical analysis is inherently incomplete and leaves other aspects of curriculum and pedagogy unexplored, hidden, silent. Thus, in examining the intersections between curriculum and pedagogy, we strive to address multiple and perhaps even contradictory forces by welcoming many and varied analytical concerns and issues. In light of this, the editors would like to actively seek papers and other products aimed at the intellectual and empirical questions inherent in the interplay among these robust forces. Autobiographical projects discussing the circuitous journey anyone career can traverse in light of research, personal reflection, external policy, and legislation would be welcomed. Along these lines, we invite articles on the nature of gender and/or sexual orientation as related to the intricacies and issues that arise in enacting curriculum as well as papers probing diversity among various populations, cultures, and social issues at home or internationally.

Finally, spiritual, philosophical, and aesthetic educational papers may serve as catalysts in the current political debate concerning legislative account-ability and the validity of the profession.

The *Journal of Curriculum and Pedagogy* recognizes that the democratic re-lationship between curriculum and pedagogy can be found through investi-gations into the experiences of teachers and students. Furthermore, we acknowledge that teaching and learning are contextualized; and therefore, curriculum studies should reflect the characteristic ambiguity of the educa-tional terrain. To this end, the editors of this journal seek to provide a vari-ety of opportunities for documenting how knowledge is constructed and expressed in myriad ways. Currently muted by the monotonic clamor of technical rationality are the playful and inspired voices of those who would join the critical conversation surrounding curriculum and pedagogy not only through disciplinary practices but also through a wide range of inter-disciplinary, transdisciplinary, non-disciplinary, and other unique multi-discursive and artistic languages.

We envision this journal as a dialogic forum through which scholars and practitioners representing various disciplines are invited to engage in oppor-tunities to see that the conversation surrounding the relationship between curriculum and pedagogy functions ethically. The *Journal of Curriculum and Pedagogy* is committed to diversified educational research. In doing so, we hope to demonstrate that any singular approach to acquiring knowledge is an epistemological travesty that threatens the foundations of a democratic education and academic freedom. It is our intention to create challenging opportunities to further an understanding of the interrelated concerns from various epistemological viewpoints by eliciting the intersections of compet-ing voices. The journal is a stage for improvisation—a lived and living con-versation working toward understanding critical issues in education. The *Journal of Curriculum and Pedagogy* will seek, pursue, and encourage scholar-ship that invites readers to consider multiple interpretations of reality and definitions of "meaningful truth." It will provide a kaleidoscope of views that represents the interdependent, interconnected reality of human educa-tion. A plurality of involvement in curriculum construction and pedagogical practices will be painted throughout. Cultural contexts demand multiple worldviews. As the reader continues on this journey, the journal will follow a prime directive in education for over two centuries: a quest for shared knowledge. A prime consideration of curriculum and pedagogy is to con-struct, deconstruct, and reconstruct types and forms of experiences in which diverse members may form a "meaningful truth" individually as well as collectively. As a result, each member would see herself or himself as a knowledge-seeker, knowledge-holder, and knowledge-constructor within the interdependent, interconnected learning community. The journal hopes to bring these multidimensional insights into the discourse of curriculum and pedagogy to be appreciated, celebrated, and enacted by all.

Finally, the *Journal of Curriculum and Pedagogy* will treat "curriculum and pedagogy" as a distinct multi-disciplinary field. We welcome contributions that theoretically clarify the complex, chaotic nature of this field. Though the journal is situated at the intersection of curriculum theory and pedagogical practice, we recognize the importance of social theory in educational artistry.

In order to extend critical discussion and advance research that situates education in these contexts, the journal goals are:

> To increase the dialogue that must exist about all educational issues to provide for the continuation of the democratic process,

> To open a public space where students, educators, educational political systems, and school cultures can "re-translate" and "re-negotiate" identities and responsibilities in the act of "educating" all members of society,

> To guide and encourage readers, using themes and topics, to engage in pedagogical theory, investigating and learning more about changing educational trends,

> To bring honest challenges to the curriculum and pedagogy in teacher preparation programs to identify problems, limitations, and conflicting realities under a socio-political scrutiny; and re-envision a socially responsible agency for public education in a democratic, pluralistic society,

> To promote non-traditional research ideology and methods that hold profound capacities for uncovering unknown voices and realities in curriculum construction and pedagogical practices,

> To provide disempowered scholars and researchers outside the dominant social order with a forum for advancement of ideology of socio-political constructs in diverse cultural contexts.

Appendix B

Transformative Curriculum Leadership: Illustrative Signposts

In general, educators who are interested in transformative curriculum leadership begin their personal 'journeys of understanding' from a customary and habitual perspective on what constitutes 'good' curriculum work. For shorthand purposes, this will be described as:

- *Customary understanding*...the journey of understanding has not yet been initiated.

As inspired, motivated educators undertake their individual journeys of understanding, they will most likely go through three overlapping and interrelated phases: emergent, engaged and generative. These phases can be briefly described as follows:

- *Emergent understanding*...there is a growing awareness of the vital importance of transformative curriculum leadership in schools with democratic missions

- *Engaged understanding*...the cultivation and refinement of the disciplined problem solving is underway.

- *Generative understanding*...experience in how to inspire other curriculum stakeholders, particularly professional peers, is being acquired.

The following illustrative 'signposts' have been created to assist inspired, motivated educators in the self- and peer-monitoring of their personalized journeys of understanding. These signposts are tied to the content in C&I 6/77001, "Fundamentals of Curriculum" and to the SPN assignment in this course. They are a limited list, and more personally relevant signposts (pertaining to each educator's individualized journey of understanding) could be added to this list. In effect, these signposts are part of an 'open set' of possibilities.

Illustrative Signposts: Customary Understanding

- My SPN indicates that I base my curriculum actions on the policy directives of external authorities and/or on the 'constructivist best practice' guidelines advanced by professional organizations. I don't clearly distinguish curriculum leadership from curriculum management and/or instructional leadership.

- My SPN indicates that my referent for 'good' curriculum work is some form of curriculum management (SM paradigm) and/or instructional leadership (CBP paradigm).

- My SPN indicates that I don't understand the distinction between the *standardized management* and *constructivist best practice* problem solving paradigms, particularly how these paradigms can be applied to Tyler's (1949) "rationale."

- My SPN indicates that I am not aware of the dominance of the reductionist, efficiency *logic* of the Tyler rationale, nor do I have knowledge of critiques of this dominant logic that are part of the curriculum studies literature.

- My SPN indicates that technical workshops are my 'horizon of understanding' for professional development.

- My SPN is limited to a discussion of my occupational responsibilities as a skilled technician.

- My SPN indicates no interest, or perhaps a very limited interest, in curriculum theorizing.

Illustrative Signposts: Emergent Understanding

- My SPN indicates that I understand that instruction is situated in a larger 'ecology' of curriculum work fundamentals.

- My SPN contains evidence that I am aware of the pros and cons of the Tyler rationale, particularly with reference to Kliebard's (1992) critique of this curriculum problem solving approach.

- My SPN indicates that I am comfortable critiquing the Tyler rationale.

- My SPN indicates that I am still acquiring a critical distance from customary curriculum/instructional practices.

- My SPN incorporates a clear explanation of the TCL transactional activity set.

- My SPN expresses my personal ambivalences about this curriculum leadership.

- My SPN suggests that I am not sure that this definition of curriculum leadership is part of my vocational calling.

- My SPN notes that I am still contemplating possibilities for engaging in this disciplined way of living.

Illustrative Signposts: Engaged Understanding

- My SPN expresses my commitment to cultivate the personal discipline that this curriculum leadership requires. I indicate that I establish a critical distance from the limitations of 'external' management discipline while developing an 'inner' problem solving discipline.

- My SPN makes reference to personal changes in my curriculum problem solving habits, which can be generally characterized as "habits of hope." Shade (2001) explains this concept:

Habits of hope are those habits by which we pursue—that is, seek and nurture—the realization of hope's ends. They are vital and integral dynamics in developing hope, particularly in maintaining our commitment to its ends. ...These habits either build connections between hope's end and our current agency or, when agency is limited, expand it generally. (p. 77)

- My SPN clearly demonstrates that I understand the difference between a professional learning community (PLC) and a *disciplined professional learning community* (DPLC).

- My SPN contains evidence of my commitment to join a DPLC that supports and sustains the curriculum leadership.

- My SPN contains evidence that I am studying and practicing the four disciplined, collaborative curriculum and teaching transactions.

Illustrative Signposts: Generative Understanding

- My SPN indicates that I am developing an identity as a curriculum worker who can influence my professional peers and other curriculum stakeholders such as students' parents.

- My SPN contains evidence of "wiggle room" deliberations (Cuban, 2003) and resourceful negotiations (Walker & Soltis, 2009) with reference to the pragmatic advancement of this definition of curriculum leadership.

- My SPN contains evidence that I am comfortable serving as an inspirational role model for the 'habits of hope' that sustains this curriculum leadership.

- My SPN includes a site-specific curriculum leadership plan of action incorporating one or more DPLC projects and PI activities.

These illustrative 'signposts' are part of an open set of personally relevant ways to monitor the 'journey of understanding' component of this curriculum leadership. There, certainly, could be other ways that this could be accomplished. Furthermore, monitoring is part of a larger set of evaluative activities. There are many other ways that educators could evaluate their professional development progress in embodying and enacting this curriculum leadership.

References

Cuban, L. (2003). *Why is it so hard to get good schools?* New York: Teachers College Press.

Kliebard, H. K. (1992). *Forging the American curriculum: Essays in curriculum history and theory.* New York: Routledge.

Shade, P. (2001). *Habits of hope: A pragmatic theory.* Nashville: Vanderbilt University Press.

Tyler, R. W. (1949). *Basic principles of curriculum and instruction.* Chicago: University of Chicago Press.

Walker, D. F., & Soltis, J. F. (2009). *Curriculum and aims* (5th ed.). New York: Teachers College Press.

Appendix C

The Professional Standard for the C&I Master's Degree Program

The standard:

> Educators will demonstrate the necessary disciplinary understanding to
> practice a resourceful and democratic curriculum-based pedagogy; and
> they will consider the possibility of serving as 'transformative' curricu-
> lum leaders for this professional artistry.

This is not a state-mandated standard tied to an external, accountability
system. It is an invitational standard grounded in personal inspiration and
guided by an internal sense of discipline.

Transformative Curriculum Leadership (TCL), which is introduced, explained and illustrated at a Kent State University "Curriculum Leadership"
website, contains a *set* of six interrelated transactional and leadership activities, which are presented in Henderson and Gornik (2007). The website
can be retrieved at: www.ehhs.kent.edu/cli . As explained and illustrated at
the website, the enactment of the TCL 'activity set' is qualitatively enhanced
by the practice of four types of *disciplined mindfulness*[1]:

- **Moral Imagination:** being mindful of the possibilities of cultivating a dynamic relationship between democracy and education; envisioning education in a deep democracy.

- **Transactional Aesthetics:** being mindful of the feel of democratic reciprocity between teacher and student, teacher and
  teacher, teacher and administrator, and any other curriculum
  stakeholder combination; attuning to the beauty of democratic
  interactions.

---

[1] The general term, "mindfulness," which allows for diverse, personal expression,
refers to a wholly-engaged attentiveness, what Dewey (1910/1933) calls "whole-
heartedness...or with a whole heart" (p. 31).

- **Deliberative Artistry:** being mindful about practicing a sensitive, nuanced decision-making that touches on each student's humanity; enacting curriculum judgments that foster deep democratic values.

- **Ethical Fidelity:** being mindful about matters of democratic integrity as expressed in curriculum mission statements; embodying deep democracy in present educational moments.

Stories, conversations and other communications about these four types of disciplined mindfulness can be viewed as "expressive outcomes" (Eisner, 1994) of ongoing personalized journeys of understanding.

References

Dewey, J. (1933). *How we think: A restatement of the relation of reflective thinking to the educative process.* Boston: D. C. Heath and Company. (Original work published 1910)

Eisner, E. W. (1994). *The educational imagination: On the design and evaluation of school programs* (3rd ed.). New York: Macmillan.

Henderson, J. G., & Gornik, R. (2007). *Transformative curriculum leadership* (3rd ed.). Upper Saddle River, NJ: Merrill/Prentice Hall.

Appendix D

A Snapshot of Your Journey of Understanding

Part I

With reference to your customary understanding of curriculum work and your interpretations of the three *phases of understanding* associated with transformative curriculum leadership, you are being asked to describe where you feel you are *positioned* on your professional development journey at this point in time. As you complete this snapshot, keep in mind that there are two general *patterns* of customary understanding: (1) a custom/habit of not making a distinction between educational management and leadership and (2) a custom/habit of not making a distinction between semi-professional and professional teaching.

1 – MY CUSTOMARY UNDERSTANDING (REVIEW YOUR BASELINE ESSAY) – summarize in 1 to 2 sentences:

2 – MY EMERGENT UNDERSTANDING – summarize in 1 to 2 sentences:

3 – MY ENGAGED UNDERSTANDING – summarize in 1 to 2 sentences:

4 – MY GENERATIVE UNDERSTANDING – summarize in 1 to 2 sentences:

Part II

Read each of the four questions below and mark on the line the point that captures your current 'journey of understanding' positioning.

Question #1 – I still feel immersed in my *Customary Understanding*

Not at All   Somewhat   A Lot

Question #2 – With reference to my interpretation of *Emergent Understanding*, I position myself in

An Early Stage   An Intermediate Stage   An Advanced Stage

Question #3 – With reference to my interpretation of *Engaged Understanding*, I position myself in

An Early Stage   An Intermediate Stage   An Advanced Stage

Question #4 – With reference to my interpretation of *Generative Understanding*, I position my in

An Early Stage   An Intermediate Stage   An Advanced Stage

Part III

Imagine your continuing growth as a TCL 'lead learner' during your master's degree work. How do you see yourself positioned with respect to your customary, emergent, engaged, and/or generative understanding of this professional leadership at the end of your graduate studies? As you respond to this question, keep in mind that your growth is a highly personalized process potentially involving a complex mix of customary, emergent, engaged, and/or generative understandings.